The Rosary of the Philosophers

of the

De Alchemia Opuscula complura veterum
philosophorum

Johann Daniel Myliu

Here beginneth the Book of the Rosary of the Philosophers most diligently compiled and brought into one volume.

They who desire to have the most true knowledge of the greater science of the philosophical Art, let them diligently peruse this little book and often times read it over and they shall obtain their prosperous and wished desire. Listen to these things, you children of the Ancient Philosophers, I will speak in the loudest and highest voice I can, for I come unto you to open and declare the principal state of human things and the most secret treasure of all the secrets of the whole world. I will not do it feignedly and erroneously but altogether plainly and truly, wherefore use you towards me such devotion of hearing as I shall bring unto you magistery of doctrine and wisdom, for I will show you a true testimony of those things which I have seen with my own eyes and felt with my hands. There are many men too forward as deceitful boasters which after great expenses and labours, find out no effect but misery. I will therefore speak plainly and manifestly so that the unskillful, as those that are expert and skilful, shall be able to understand the secret of this mystery. Neither shall any man justly use slanderous and blasphemous words against me, for seeing that the Ancient Philosophers have written so obscurely and confusedly that they are not understood, nor seem not to agree together, because diverse men searching after this most precious Art have either been deceived or terrified from their purpose, therefore without all deceit or obscurity, I will plainly set down the true experiment before your eyes, together with the opinions of the Philosophers, serving well for our purpose that the matter whereof we entreat may be manifest and plainly understood.

First we must note that all men which work beyond nature are deceivers and work in an unlawful manner. Furthermore, of man nothing is born but man, and of a brute beast nothing but a brute beast, and every like bringeth forth nothing but his like, wherefore he which have not of his own, cannot at his pleasure have another man's. We speak this that no man should let his money go from him. For some men being deceived by letting their money pass from them, and so living in penury, do also endeavour to seduce other men and to bring them to like misery. But my counsel is that no man be too forward in this art, in hope to attain some great matter, unless he knows the beginning of true nature and the regimen thereof, which being known there is not then any need of more things than one, neither doth it require great expenses, because it is one stone, one medicine, one vessel, one regimen, and one disposition, and know this: that it is a most true Art. Furthermore the Philosophers would never have laboured and studied to express such diversities of colours and the order of them unless they had seen and felt them.

Wherefore again we say this, that all men labouring beyond nature are deceivers and deceived. Therefore let your exercise and labour be used in Nature because Our Stone is of an Animal, of a Vegetable, and of a Mineral substance. Be thou therefore of one mind and opinion in the work of nature and presume not to try this thing here and that thing another time, for our Art is not effected with the multitude of things and though the names thereof be diverse and manifold, yet it is always one only thing and of one thing. For that is not brought into nature which being in it is not of its own nature, therefore it is necessary that the Agent and Patient be One thing, and the same thing in kind or in general, but in species another and diverse, according to Mercury by which the woman is diversified from the man, because, although they agree in one kind, yet they have a distinct difference between themselves, as Matter and Form differ, for Matter suffers action but Form works and makes the Matter like itself. Therefore, Matter naturally desires Form, as the woman does the man, and the foul does the fair, so the body embraceth the spirit more freely that it may come to its perfection. Therefore, by knowing the natural roots you shall the better make your work of them. Because I cannot any other way express or explain our stone, nor form it by any other name, it is manifest by that which went before, that our stone is compounded of four elements, both rich and poor have it, and it is found in every place, it is likened to all things and is also compounded of body, soul and spirit and it is altered from nature into nature even to the last degree of his perfection.

They have also said that our stone is made of one thing and it is true for the whole magistery is done with our water, for that water is the sperm of all metals, and all metals are resolved into it, as has been declared.

Likewise, the salt of metals is the stone of the Philosophers, for our stone is a water congealed into Gold and Silver and resists the fire and is resolved again into its water of which it is compounded in its kind. Therefore, the reduction of bodies into their first matter as into Argent vive is nothing else but a resolution of the congealed matter by which a lock is opened by the ingression of one nature into another.

Whereupon, the Philosophers have said that Sol is nothing else but ripened Argent vive, for in Mercury there are but two elements in act, that is to say earth and water which are passives, but the active elements as air and fire are in that might and power only because those things are brought from power into act in pure Mercury according to due digestion and proportionable decoction, then Gold is made. Wherefore there are four elements in Gold made fit in equal proportion and therefore ripe and active Sulphur is there, and our Art helpeth nature by her ministering ripe Gold to Mercury, in which is ripe and well digested Sulphur, but from nature by the work of nature.

Arnoldus: Whosoever would come to the knowledge of this Art and is not a Philosopher will prove a fool, because this Science is only of the Secrets of Philosophers.

Senior: This Art is reserved in the power of God and is an enemy to the lay people.

Geber: Therefore this Art is not necessary for poor and needy men but is rather an enemy to them.

Aristotle in the Second Book of his Politics: It is impossible for a poor man to be a Philosopher.

There is a double way in this art according to the Philosophers, that is - universal and particular. The universal way is easy and rare, and it is that which is brought forth from true and natural beginnings, by which a speedy and reformative virtue doth presently and in a moment hardens Mercury, and it tinctureth any metal that is duly prepared, into true Gold or Silver.

But the second way is called particular and it is hard and laboursome. Note this, although Alchemy in the universal way be partly natural and partly artificial, yet it is more natural than otherwise, because by nature no strange or foreign thing is brought in the way of true Alchemy, for nature hath whereon to work because actives are joined to passives by a competent union and application, but the rest nature worketh by herself.

Plato: Our stone is a thing which hath not touched the fire, nor the fire touched it, from which our mercury riseth.

There are three sorts of labourers according to the art of Alchemy, that is the Alchimist, the Lauchimist, and the Lachrymist. Not every one who sayeth "Take, Take", shall enter into this art, because it is one only receipt, and one body entereth not into another.

Gratianus: Take this and this and do thus and thus, and you shall have this, and this is a common thing among all Philosophers.

Whereupon the Philosopher said, the first word, "Take, Take", hath made many errors, therefore, the first work is to dissolve the matter of the stone, that is, not common Mercury.

Arnoldus: Fools understanding the sayings of the Philosophers according to the letter do find out no truth, and they say it is a false science because they have tried it and found nothing, and then they become as men desperate, condemning this science and dispraising the books thereof, and therefore the science maketh small account of them, because our science of the secrets of nature hath no enemy but the ignorant, according to these verses following:

This stone is had in small regard
With men of slender wit
But yet the wise and learned sort
Make great account of it.

Alphidius: Know this, that God hath not ordained this stone of which this great secret entreateth to be bought for a great price, for it is found out being cast in the way, and may as well be had of a poor man as of a rich man, that every man may come unto it by reason and knowledge. Argent vive is not the stone, whereupon Constantinus saith "Because it is fusible, therefore it is not the stone".

Argent vive is fire whereupon the Philosopher said, "Know therefore that Argent vive is fire and burns bodies more than fire".

We are the beginning and first nature of metals,
Art by us maketh the chief tincture.
There is no fountain nor water found like unto me.
I heal and help both the rich and the poor,
But yet I am full of hurtful poison.

The juices of Lunaria, Aqua Vitae, Fifth Essence, Spirit of wine, mercury vegetable, are all one. The juices of Lunaria is made of our wine, which thing is known but to few of our children, and with it is our solution made, and our potable gold is made, that being the mean thereof and cannot be without it.

For the imperfect body is converted into the first matter, and those waters being conjoined with our water do make one pure and clear water, purifying all things and yet containing in itself all necessary things. And this water of which and with which our magistery is effected, is both dear and cheap, for it dissolveth bodies not with common solution as the ignorant report, which converts the body into cloud water, but by the true philosophical solution, in which the body is changed into its first water of which it hath been from the beginning this self same body. That is, the water transforms bodies into Ashes. But know this, that the Art of Alchemy is a gift of the Holy Ghost and know that in our days we have had Master Arnold de Villa Nova in the Roman Court, a great Physician and Divine, who hath also been a notable Alchimist, who made small wedges of gold which wedges he granted to be put to any trial.

Arnoldus: Let the Artificers of Alchemy know this, that the forms of metals cannot be transmuted unless they be reduced into their first matter, and then they are transmuted into another form than that which they had before. And that is because the corruption of one thing is the generation of another thing, as well in artificial things as in natural things. For Art imitates nature and in certain things it correcteth it and excelleth it as nature is helped by the industry of the Physician.

The Mirror: Therefore, use nature well because nature cannot be amended but in its own nature, to which bring in no foreign thing, neither powder, nor any other thing, because diverse natures do not make perfect the stone, neither does that enter into it which is not sprung from it. For if any foreign or strange thing be put into it, it is straight corrupted and that which is sought shall not be obtained.

Whereupon, I give you to understand that, unless you take like things in the beginning of the decocting and guide them subtly until they all be made water, till then you have not found out the work. Wherefore, I will make the precious secret known unto the students thereof, they they shall not be wearied in vain, because this magistery is nothing else but to decoct Argent vive and Sulphur, until the Argent vive be made all one, which defendeth the Sulphur from burning if the vessel be well closed, so that the Argent vive may not vanish away nor the Sulphur be burned or consumed, because our Argent vive is our pure water. And we see the example in common water, that every thing which is decocted in it is never burnt till the water is consumed and the fire be very strong, and when the water is consumed, then that which is in the vessel is burnt. And therefore, the Philosophers have willed us to stop the mouth of the vessel close, that our blessed water breath not forth, but that it may defend that from burning which is in the vessel, but water being put with these things doth forbid the fire to burn them, and then those things are done and made. And the greater the flame is, yet so much the more be hidden in the inward parts, that it be not hurt by the heat of the fire. The water receiveth them in his belly and repelleth the flame of the fire from them. But I would wish all the searchers after this Art, in the beginning to make a soft fire, till patience be made between the water and the fire, and after you shall see the water fixed without any ascending, then you need not care in what sort the fire be, but yet it is good to govern it with patience, till the spirit and body be made all one, so that the corporate bodies be made incorporate, and the incorporate be made corporate. Therefore, water is the thing which maketh white and red. It is the water which killeth and reviveth. It is the water which burneth and maketh hot. It is the water which dissolveth and congealeth. It is the water which putrefieth and afterwards causeth new and contrary things to spring up. Wherefore, my son, I counsel thee that all thy labour and diligence be used in the decocting of the water. And let it not be irksome unto thee if thou desire to have the fruit thereof and take care for no other vain matters, but for water only. Decoct that water by little and little, by putrefying until it be changed from colour into a perfect colour, and take care that in the beginning you burn not the flowers and greenness thereof, and be not too hasty in bringing your work to pass, and remember that your door be well and firmly shut, that he which is within fly not out and thus by the help of God you shall obtain a wished effect. Nature makes her operation by little and little, therefore, I would also that you should do so, yea rather let your imagination be according to nature, and see according to nature, of which bodies are regenerated according to nature in the bowels of the earth. Imagine this by true imagination and not phantastically and likewise see in what colour the decoction of them is made, in whether it be violent or pleasant.

Geber - Of the Investigation of Truth

We have considered in our volumes of the secret and natural powers and of the properties of natural things, and by our own experience of the invention of the searching out of a matter altogether certain. We have not found out any other thing but only those things of which our medicine is made, that it may have these properties in itself in transmuting of bodies.

First, that it may have a most subtle earth in itself, and incombustible and apt to fix anything with its own radical moisture.

Secondly, that it may have an airy and fiery moisture uniformly conjoined, so that if one be volatile the rest may be so also, and because that moisture above all other moistures abideth all other moistures, to the accomplishment of this sufficient thickness of ashes so far forth as the want thereof, with an unseparable permanency of the earth that is annexed without evaporation.

Thirdly, because the natural disposition of moisture is such that by the benefit of its homogeneity it hath in all differences of its properties, annexed earth by the conversion of them both, because in the homogeneity of either of them it is tempered virtuously with an inseparable bond of conjoining, and after the degree of final preparation it yieldeth good melting.

Fourthly, that this homogeneity is of such purity of Essence and artificially purified from all combustible and burnt substance, that all things which are joined with it are not burnt by it, but it preserveth them from burning.

Fifthly, because it hath a clear and bright tincture in itself, white, red, pure, incombustible, stable and fixed, which neither the fire is able to change nor burnt sulphurs or sharp corrosives able to corrupt.

Sixthly, because the whole engrafted compound with its final accomplishment is of such subtlety and thinness of substance, that after the final injection of the term of its decoction, it remaineth of most thin melting, in manner of water, and profound penetration even to the permutability of the last thing, of what fusion or melting so ever it be in the accomplishment, and cleaveth naturally to its fume with its affinity and nearness, and with inseparable hardness against the impression of the fire, even in its hour reducing bodies spiritually into its own nature.

These things being considered, we find by our investigation seven necessary and convenient properties in our stone; Oiliness, Thinness, Affinity of Substance, Radical Moisture, Purity, Clearness, Fixing Earth and Tincture.

But the first property of differences is that oiliness giving in projection a universal melting and opening of the medicine. For surely the sudden and convenient fusion of the medicine is chiefly necessary after the projection of the medicine which is done and miscerated with natural oiliness.

The second is the thinness of the matter or the spiritual subtlety thereof, thin and flowing in fusion, like water penetrating to the bottom of an altering thing, because secondly after the fusion of the medicine, the ingression thereof is immediately necessary.

The third is affinity or nearness between the Elixir and the thing to be transmuted, yielding a certain sticking or holding in the meeting of its like, because thirdly after the ingression of the medicine, the sticking or holding is convenient and necessary.

The fourth is radical moisture and fiery congealing, and hardening the refined parts with the adherence of their like and with an inseparable union of all like parts, because fourthly after the adherence or sticking, the hardening or solidifying of parts with its radical and slimy moisture is convenient and necessary.

The fifth is purity and mundified clearness, giving an eminent brightness and splendour in the present combustion, not to those joined after the hardening of the purified parts which are left, because the agent and actual fire may have sufficient to burn all foreign and hardened superfluities, wherefore putrefaction followeth immediately and is very necessary.

The sixth is fixed earth, temperate, thin, subtle, fixed, incombustible, giving permanency of fixation, sticking in solution, standing with itself and persevering against the fire, because sixthly, fixation is necessary after purification.

The seventh is tincture, giving a bright and perfect colour, white and deep red, giving the lunification and solification of transmutable things, because seventhly the just tincting colour or tincture is necessary after fixation, turning any convertible substance into true gold and silver, with all its certain and known differences.

Calidus the Philosopher speaks of our water: For it is a fire which burneth and grindeth all things, Argent vive is vinegar.

Socrates in the Turba: "The first force is vinegar, that is Argent vive.

Turba: If you set the body on the fire without vinegar, it will be burnt, that is without Argent vive ... It is most sharp vinegar which maketh the mere body without which no colour cometh.

Note well in the art of our magistery, nothing is concealed of the Philosophers, except the secret of the art, which is not lawful to be revealed to any man, for he that should do so would be accursed, and incur the indignation of the Lord and die with the palsy. Wherefore, all error is in the art, because they take not their due matter out of it, therefore use reverent nature; of it, by it, and in it, our art is engendered and in no other thing, and therefore our magistery is a work of nature and not of a workman. And so he which knoweth not the beginning, obtaineth not the end, and he which knoweth not what he seeks is ignorant also what he shall find.

Know therefore that copper, which is the gold of the Philosophers, is their gold, but Senior said "Our gold is not common gold". And you have sought after the greenness, thinking that copper had been a leprous body by reason of that greenness which it hath. Whereupon, I tell you that all that is perfect in copper is only that greenness which is in it, because that greenness is by our magistery quickly turned into our most pure gold, and this we have tried, but you can by no means prepare the stone without green and liquid Duenech, which is seen to grow in our minerals. O blessed greenness, which engenders all things. You know that no vegetable and fruit appeareth in growing but it is of a green colour. Know therefore, that the generation of this thing is green, wherefore the Philosophers have called it their growing or springing. And likewise, they have called it water of their purification or putrefaction, and they spoke the truth, because it is purified by their water or purified from its blackness. It is washed and it maketh it white and afterwards red. Know therefore, that there is no true tincture, but of our Copper, decoct it therefore with his soul, grind it, and do thus, until the spirit be conjoined with his body and be made in one, and you shall have your desire. The wisemen have given many names to it, but consider you only of that matter which sticketh to Argent vive and to the bodies, and you shall have the true knowledge and science. But that you may not err, know therefore what it is to stick in the bodies. Some have said that common Argent vive sticketh in the bodies, which is false. For they think that they understand the chapter of Geber intimating of Argent vive, where he saith, "When we search in other things, we find out by our searching nothing to be more friendly to the nature of bodies than Argent vive". But all this must be understood of the philosophical Argent vive, for it only sticketh in bodies, and the ancient Philosophers could find out no other thing which would stick to the bodies but philosophical Argent vive, because common silver sticketh not in the bodies, but rather the bodies cleave and stick to Argent vive. And this is true by experience, because if common Argent vive be conjoined with any body, the Argent vive remaineth in its own nature, or goeth away and does not turn the body into its nature. And therefore, it sticketh not unto the bodies but the bodies cleave and stick to it, and by reason of this many men are deceived in working in that common Argent vive, because it is clear our occidental stone exceeding Argent vive, which hath preferred itself before gold and hath overcome it, is that which killeth and causeth to revive again. Know therefore, that Argent vive coagulated and mortified in his own nature, is the father of all the miracles of this our magistery, and it is a spirit and a body, that is a spiritual body, because it ascends by sublimation. And this is because Geber said the consideration of the true thing which doeth all things, is the consideration of the choice of the pure substance of Argent vive, but of which especially this substance of Argent vive may be chosen, that must diligently be sought after. And we answering say that it is chosen out of those things in which it is.

Therefore my son, consider and see where that substance is, and take that and none other if you desire to come to the true understanding. I tell thee in the charity of Christ that neither we nor the ancient Philosophers could ever find any thing persevering and abiding in the fire, but only that unctuous, perfect and combustible moisture, and that moisture when it is prepared as it ought to be, it bringeth all bodies which it touches to a most true compliment of gold, and above all bodies and especially Luna.

The root of the art is the soap of the wisemen, and it is the mineral of all salts and it is called bitter salt, because it cometh of the mineral of the sea, and it is more sharp than all salts of its kind. Bodies and spirits are calcined with it and the resolutions and coagulations of Elixir are made with it.

Geber: Note this that no silver can be made unless first they be all dissolved.

Secondly, that no solution ought to be made but in the proper and appropriated blood, that is, in water of Mercury which is called Dragon's Water.

Thirdly, that no Dragon Water ought to be made by an alembic, without any other thing added, and in the making of it there is a great stink.

Fourthly, that with that body of water an Amalgam may be dissolved, as also a body, a spirit and briefly all things in general, which are of its nature.

Fifthly, that that water ought to be pure and clean, and therefore should not be made but of a purged Dragon. And let the Dragon be purged by elevating it three times and then by reviving it.

Sixthly, that the dissolved must be purified in warm and moist, that is in horse dung. Of this one blackness riseth.

Seventhly, that it be coagulated in the dry Sun, in moisture that is in Balneo Maria.

Eighthly, that the time of the perfection of Elixir is less than one year, yet we must see that it be the time of the increase of man in the womb of the mother.

Ninthly, that Mercury is by no means killed, but with the smell of the body, perfected red to red and of white to white. And that the body can give weight, his own weight remaining, there are four things with which our work is effected, that is Weight, Fire, Body and Spirit.

Tenthly, that all revived things are not to be refused in the Art.

Eleventhly, that the thing being prepared and put in the vessel, it will then be women's work and children's play, because the magistery may be done in one vessel. Likewise, whosoever hath true Mercury, hath Elixir also, because Elixir is mortified Mercury, or fixed with the smell of the body, because the Dragon dieth not but with his brother and sister. Note likewise, that Mercury must altogether be made of the body, that is, that fixed be made volatile with volatile, that is with pure Mercury. And it is needful that there be more of the volatile than of the fixed, from double to fivefold to sixfold unto tenfold, and no further, and the more volatile parts there are, so much the more slowly are they fixed, and the fixed is made volatile in the space of one month. And note that, Elixir cannot be unless the body and spirit pass through all the Elements. That is, through all natures of Elements, that first they may be made earth, afterwards air, that is vapour, thirdly water, and fourthly fire, for everything is called fire which doth not fly the fire, nor diminish nor consume in the fire.

He that will search out the secret of this Art must know the first matter of our bodies, for otherwise he shall spend his labour in vain.

The first matter of bodies is not common mercury, but it is an unctuous and moist vapour. For of the moist the mineral stone is made, and of the unctuousness the metallic body. For it is meet that the bodies be converted into such an unctuous vapour, and in the conversion the bodies are killed and the grain [seed] of the body is overthrown with death and altogether mortified, and this is done by the aid of our white and red water. And understand it, that unless the grain of Corn, that is the grain of the body, be cast into the earth, that is into its first water, which is an unctuous vapour or the mercury of the wise men and of the Philosophers, and such a vapour is called the known Stone in the chapters of books, and the beginning of the matter of our operation, and unctuous sulphur out of which the Fifth Essence is extracted, in the accomplishment Mercury tinctureth every body into Sol and Luna, according to which way the Stone hath been finally prepared. Note likewise, that although all ancient wise men of Alchemy have spoken many things and conclude of Salt, and because they speak of the Soap of the Wise and the Key that shutteth and openeth and shutteth again and no man openeth without this Key, they say that no man in this world can come to the perfection of this Science unless he know to calcine Salt after its preparation. And they say that it must be in a temperate place the space of three days, that the heat of the fire and the fumes may evaporate away. And therefore I conclude of this, that every good and perfect medicine of Alchemy and Elixir or powder must be in manner of Salt, and be Salt itself, and have the virtue of Salt in being of slow fusion and penetrating when cast on the bodies of melted or fiery metals. And of this Geber warneth us when he sayeth "It is necessary that the medicine be of a more speedy melting than Mercury, so that it may sooner melt before the flight of Mercury, and that the fire may not consume nor destroy it, and then it is called fusible salt and incombustible oil, and the Soap of the Wise."

Note likewise, that the Salt of metals transmuteth Mercury into true Sol and Luna and thus the Salt of Animals transmuteth every animal into true temperance and a good complexion. The fire of dung is the agent cause in the work of the Digestion of our Stone, neither is the fire of Balneo Maria of any force, although it be most temperate in the place thereof.

Alphidius: To decoct that in fire which I shall show unto thee, is to bury it in moist horse dung, because the fire of wise men is moist and obscure, and it is warm in the second degree and moist in the first degree. The property of this fire is not to destroy oil that is the substance, but it augmenteth by reason of this temperate moisture for that heat only is equal and temperate, and such is very necessary in the generation of that thing.

Geber: Because the fumes are most subtle and have need of temperate decoction, that they may be thickened in themselves, according to the equality for temperate heat only, is the thickening of moistness and perfection of mixture, and not exceeding too far, for the generations and procreations of natural things have been accustomed to be done by most temperate and equal heat, as horse dung only is moist and warm.

Hermes The Fourth Book of Treatises: It behoveth him who would enter into this art and secret wisdom to repel the vice of arrogancy from him, and to become virtuous and honest and profound in reason, courteous unto men, merry and pleasant of countenance, patient and a concealer of secrets. My Son, before all things I counsel thee to fear God, in whom the sight of thy disposition remains, and the help of every thing sequestered from thee.

Geber - The Book of Perfect Magistery: It is necessary for the Artificer of this science to be most subtle of wit, and to know and understand the natures of metals and their generations, infirmities and imperfections in their minerals, before he can come to this Art. Let no workman come to search out this Art, being loaded with gross and dull wit, or being sparing or covetous in his expenses, nor any man of double or variable mind, either over-happy or captious, but the Son of Learning imbued with a subtle and politic wit, sufficiently rich, bountiful, healthful, firm and constant in his purpose, patient, gentle, long-suffering and temperate.

Alphidius: Know, My Son, that thou canst not obtain this science until thou purify thy mind onto God, and till God knoweth thee to have a staid and upright mind, and then he will make thee to reign and rule over the world.

Aristotle: If God knew there were a faithful mind in man, he would then reveal this Secret unto him.

The Correction of the Ignorant: It is necessary for every Art to imitate the Scoria, and to understand the nature thereof, and thus art imitates his nature. Know, ignorant man, that by Art nature itself is known and cannot be amended, and of necessity the follower of nature must come to a perfect end of the Secrets of the Philosophers.

Hermes and Geber: He which shall once bring this Art to a full end if he should live a thousand years, and should every day nourish four thousand men, yet he should never want.

Senior: He is so rich which hath the stone whereof Elixir is made, as he which hath fire may give fire to whom he will, when he will, and as much as he will without any peril or want unto himself.

The Table of the Greater Science
First there is had in our Green Lion the true matter, and of what colour it is, and is called Adrop, Azoth, or Duenech virid.
In the second there is likewise had, as in the third chapter, how bodies are dissolved into philosophical argent vive, that is into water of our mercury, and it is made one new body.
In the fourth, the putrefaction of the philosophers is had, which hath never been seen in our days, and it is called Sulphur.
In the fifth, is had how the great part of this water is made black and feculent earth whereof all philosophers speak.
In the sixth, is had how that black earth stood in the beginning above

the water, and how by little and little it hath been drowned in the bottom of the vessel.

In the seventh, is had how that earth is dissolved again into water in the colour of oil, and then it is called the Oil of the Philosophers.

In the eighth, is had how the Dragon is born in his blackness and is fed with his Mercury, and killeth himself and is drowned in it, and the water is somewhat whitened, and that is Elixir.

In the ninth, is had how the water is wholly purified from his blackness and remains the colour of milk, and many colours appear in the blackness.

In the tenth, is had how those black clouds which were in the vessel above the water, descended into their body from whence they came.

In the eleventh, is had how that ashes is made most white, like glistening marble, and that is White Elixir, and the increase is ashes.

In the twelfth, is had how that whiteness is converted into redness like a ruby, and that is Red Elixir.

And if thou wilt understand the whole work perfectly, then read one part after another and thou shall see miracles.

I have seen all these things in my days, even to the Lion. I have not spoken of all things which are appertaining and necessary to this work because there are some things which men may not speak of. And it is impossible to know this art unless it be known of God, or of a Master who may touch Him. And know that this is a very long way, therefore patience is necessary in this our magistery. Argent vive is common salt.

Rosarius: Common salt dissolveth gold and silver, and it augmenteth redness in Gold and whiteness in Silver, and it changeth Copper from his corporality to spirituality, and therewith are bodies calcined.

Light of Lights: If the omnipotent God had not created this salt, Elixir could not have been effected, and the study of Alchemy had been but lost labour.

Note this, there are four Mercuries— Crude Mercury, Sublimed Mercury, Mercury of Magnesia, and Unctuous Mercury. But Mercury is full of Luna: Mercury of the Philosophers, that is the substance in which the Mercury of the Philosophers is contained. And it is that which nature hath but little worked and framed it into a metallic form, and yet he hath left it imperfect. Thus we must note that it is such a thing which is called the middle of Ingression, which is neither perfect nor altogether imperfect. Because, of nothing, nothing can be made, and because nature hath not finished in it, therefore the workman may reduce it from imperfection to perfection, by helping nature itself, and that is called the Stone of Invisibleness, the Holy Stone, the Blessed Thing.

Geber: Argent vive hath no adustion, therefore its purifying is a renewing of its earthiness and wateriness by policy, which if it be pure, it will coagulate that strength of white Sulphur not burning, into Silver, and this is so excellent a thing that by workmanship Elixir may be made of it for Silver, but if it be excellent red Sulphur of a nature not burning, then it is so notable a thing that Elixir for Gold may be made of it. Such Sulphur is our Sulphur, and the Sulphur of the Wise, and it is not found out above the earth, unless it be extracted out of these bodies.

Arnoldus: Sulphur which is hidden in Argent vive is a thing giving a golden form to that Argent vive by the virtue of the colour of his outward mineral Sulphur.

Avicenna: Such sulphur is not found on the earth, but that which is in bodies, therefore let these bodies be subtly prepared that we may have Sulphur on the earth, for a perfect body by our magistery, helpeth and bringeth to pass an imperfect thing, without the mixture of any other strength or foreign thing. For otherwise the Sulphur of what kind soever it be, will hinder the true melting, as is manifest in Iron which melteth not, because it is known to have fixed Sulphur in it. And though it be not fixed but taketh right melting, yet it is hindred and burnt of the fire, and doth evaporate away, as is manifest in Lead, and in other infirm bodies. Therefore, common Sulphur is not of the truth of our Art, nor of its perfection, because it hindreth the perfect in all its operations.

Geber: Sulphur can never be fixed unless it be first calcined, and when it is calcined, it yieldeth no fusion or melting.

Senior: Sulphur and Arsenic are not the true medicine of this magistery, because they neither accomplish nor effect fully, as hath been sufficiently known of all the lesser minerals.

Albertus: The property of Sulphur is to congeal Mercury and to bring it to pass or make it perfect with Mercury, but tincture only consisteth of two perfect bodies out of which those Sulphurs may be chosen.

The Philosopher: The foundation of this art is Sol and his shadow.

Morienus: Three forms suffice for the whole magistery that is white fume, that is the first force, that is to say celestial water, and the Green Lion, which is the Copper of Hermes, and stinking water, which is the mother of all metals, of the which, by the which, and with the which, the Philosophers prepare Elixir in the beginning and the end. Therefore conceal from no man these three forms to the perfection thereof, but a fool handleth this magistery about every other thing.

Hermes: Philosophy hath three parts, that is to say, Sol, Luna and Mercury. Of those being joined together, father Hermes knew how to make tincture.

Johannes of Aquino: He which knoweth not the destruction of Gold, cannot know the making thereof, by the necessary course of nature, so that it is more easy to make Gold than to destroy it, but he who believing to bring tincture to a wished end without those things, proceedeth blindly in practise, as an ass to his supper, because the body passeth not into the body, nor the spirit into the spirit, for form receives neither impression of form, nor matter of matter, because like hath no action nor passion in his like, when no one of them is more worthy than the other, because like hath no rule or government over like.

Aristotle: There is no true generation, but of things agreeing in nature, because the things are not done but according to their nature, for the willow never bringeth forth pears, nor the bush good pomegranates, neither can an evil tree make good fruit.

The Philosopher: Our Mercury is converted into every nature or natures, with which it shall be joined or coupled.

The Philosopher: He who knows to destroy Gold, that it shall be no more Gold, attains to the greatest secret.

Another Philosopher: It is a hard thing for Gold to be destroyed, but most hard to be made. It is more easy to destroy accidentally than essentially.

Gold is altogether Mercury, which is manifest by the weight thereof, and by the easy combination of that Mercury. Therefore, the total and radical intention of the Philosophers is in it, for it hath obtained these virtues and excellencies, by the help of the celestial heat and motion of the planets, which by themselves is impossible to increase. But a workman if he begins this work, may attain to all these things in Mercury, by meditation and help of the fire and by policy which is the abandoner of Labour.

Albertus: It is manifest that much quantity of Argent vive is the cause of perfection in bodies, but much sulphureity is the cause of [im]perfection and corruption.

Euclides, (that most wise man): We should not work anything but in Sol and Mercury joined together, of which the Stone of the Philosophers consists. Of perfection, nothing is made because it is already perfect, as we have an example in bread. Leavened bread is perfect in its state and essence, and cometh to its last end, neither can more be leavened by it, as it is in Gold. Pure Gold is brought by the trial of the fire into a firm and fixed body, and it is impossible for the Philosophers to ferment or leaven any more with it, unless the first matter of metals be had, in which Gold may be resolved into his first matter, and into the mingled elements. Let us therefore, take that matter whereupon Gold shall be made, and by the help of workmanship be brought into the true ferment of Philosophers, and by policy, we may change this into a perfect substance, or into the spirit of perfect bodies, wherefore, ever many Philosophers labouring herein are deceived, because they leave off the work, where it should be begun. O ye Sons of Learning who hope to gather the fruit before it be ripe, and hope to mow before the harvest comes.

Another Philosopher: Of that which is perfect nothing can be done or made, because the perfect forms of things are not changed in their nature but rather corrupted. Nor of a thing altogether imperfect, can any thing be made according to Art. The reason is because art cannot induce the first dispositions but our Stone is a middle thing between perfect and imperfect bodies, and what nature itself has begun, that is brought to perfection by Art. And if thou begin to work in Mercury itself, where nature hath left it imperfect, thou shall find perfection and shall rejoice. That which is perfect is not altered, but is corrupted, but an imperfect thing may be well altered. Therefore, the corruption of one thing is the generation of another thing.

Speculum: Our Stone must of necessity be extracted from the nature of two bodies before the accomplishment of the Elixir can be made of it, because it is necessary that Elixir be more purged and digested than Gold or Silver, because it must convert it altogether from his diminished perfection, into the Gold or Silver of the Philosophers, which those cannot bring to pass. For if they should give of their perfection unto another, those would remain imperfect, by reason that they cannot tinct but as much as they show themselves. Because nothing whiteneth but according to its own whiteness, neither doth anything make red but according to its own redness. And therefore, according to this the works in our Stone are done, that the tincture may be more bettered in it than in its nature, and that the Elixir may be made according to the allegory of wise men, of clear forms, treacle, medicine, and purgation of all bodies, to be purged and transformed into true Silver and Gold.

Hermes: There is the conjunction of two bodies made, and it is necessary in our magistery, and if but one of our two bodies only should be in our Stone, it would never give tincture by any means.

Therefore the Philosopher sayeth, "The wind hath carried him in his belly", wherefore it is manifest, the wind is the air, and the air is the Life, and the Life is the Soul, that is, oil and water.

Arnoldus: Trial declares the orders between the mean quantity of the fire, because in the Dissolving, the fire should be light always, in the Sublimation mean, in the Coagulation temperate, continual in the Whitening, and strong in the Rubification. But if thou err ignorantly in these points, thou will often bewail thy hard hap [luck] and lost Labour. Therefore it is necessary that you diligently follow the work because Art is helped by Policy, and likewise Policy by Art, give attendance to the accomplishment only and let other things pass.

St. Thomas of Aquinas: The matter of the Stone is a thick water, but the heat or cold, is the agent congealing that water. And assure yourself that the stones which proceed from Animals, are much more precious than other stones.

Light of Lights: No kind of stones can be prepared without Duenech, the Green and liquid, because it is of a force and engendered in our minerals.

Rasis: My Son, behold the most highest worldly things which are from the right hand and the left hand, and ascend thither where our Stone is found, and in that mountain which bringeth forth all kind of Sulphurs and shapes and likewise minerals.

Malchamech: The Stone which is necessary in this work is of a thing having life. You shall find this Stone everywhere, in plains, mountains and in waters, and both the poor and the rich have it. It is most cheap and most dear, it increaseth of flask and blood, and most precious to the man who hath it and knoweth it.

The Philosophers have said, that our Stone is of a spirit, soul and body, and they say the truth, for they have called the imperfect body-a body, ferment - the soul, and water- the spirit. And they have truly called them so, for the imperfect body by itself is a grievous body, weak and dead; water is the spirit purging the body, making it subtle and white; ferment is the soul which giveth life to the imperfect body, which life it had not before and bringeth it into a better form. The body is Venus and the woman; the Spirit is Mercury and the man; the soul is Sol and Luna. The Body must melt into his first matter which is Mercury.

Morienus: Our Mercury is not had but out of melted bodies, not with common liquefaction but only with that which endureth till the man and wife be associated and united in true matrimony and this even unto whiteness.

Morienus: Take phlegmatic and choleric blood and grind them, until the blood be made tincturing heaven.

Hermes: Understand, you sons of wisdom, that this precious Stone crieth out saying, defend me and I will defend thee, give me my right that I may help thee, for Sol is mine and the beams thereof are my inward parts; but Luna is proper to me, and my light excelleth all light, and my goods are higher than all goods. I give much riches and delights to men desiring them, and when I seek after anything they acknowledge it, I make them understand and I cause them to possess divine strength. I engender light, but my nature is darkness. Unless my metal should be dry, all bodies have need of me, because I moisten them. I blot out their rustiness and extract their substance. Therefore I and my son being joined together, there can be nothing made more better nor more honourable in the whole world.

The Disposition of the Vessel fit for our work According to the tradition of one Ferrarius by name.

Make a round glass vessel and let the bottom be of a small quantity in the manner of a little dish, and in the middle thereof, let there be a brim with an earthen girdle or ring encompassing it about, and let a round wall be built upon that girdle equally distant from the wall of the shell, of the thickness of the cover of that shell, so that in this distance the wall of the cover may fall largely without any thrusting down, but let the height of this wall be according to the height of the wall of the shell, or somewhat more or less. Let there be two covers made according to the measure of this hollowness and let the length be equal and the breadth of two great hands, and the shape of one of them like a pyramid. And in the heads of them let there be two equal holes, that the one may be in the one and the other in the other into both which a hen's feather may fall, but the whole intention of the vessel is that the cover thereof may be removed according to the will of the workman. The special intention concerning this is that the lower hollow place with its brims, enter into its cover even to the middle.

Hermes: The Dragon dieth not unless he be killed with his Brother and Sister, not by one only, but by both together, that is by Sol and Luna.

The Philosopher: Mercury never dieth unless he be killed by his Brother and Sister, that is, we must congeal it with Sol and Luna.

Note that, the Dragon is Argent vive, extracted out of bodies, having a body in himself, a soul and a spirit. Whereupon he saith, "The Dragon dieth not but with his Brother and Sister", that is with Sol and Luna, which is extracted Sulphur, having in itself the nature of moisture and coldness by reason of Luna. The Dragon dies with them - that is, Argent vive extracted from those bodies in the beginning, which is the Permanent Water of the Philosophers, which is made after the putrefaction and separation of the elements, and the water otherwise is called Stinking Water.

Bonellus: The Copper which before I spoke of is neither copper nor common tin, but it is our true work, because it must be mingled with the body of Magnesia that it may be decocted and grinded with aqua vitae, until it be destroyed. But you Sons of Learning, you must have much water, and that continually, until you have put it by parts and that the greatest part of the earth be dissolved.

Avicenna: That which is spiritual, ascendeth upwards in the vessel, but that which is thick and gross, remaineth downwards in the vessel, and unless you deal with the body in this sort, until the water will not be mingled with it, or be received of the earth, you shall but lose your labour. Therefore, unless you turn all into spiritual powder, you have not yet contrived it, i.e. grinded it, and that which you do in the white body do likewise in the red, because this medicine is

Of the Salt of the Philosophers

There are three Stones and three Salts, of which the whole magistery consists, that is to say Mineral, Plant and Animal, and there are three waters, that is of Sol, of Luna, and of Mercury. Mercury is an Mineral, Luna a plant, because it receiveth in itself two Colours, Whiteness and Redness, and Sol is an Animal because it receiveth three things, that is, Constriction, Whiteness, and Redness. And Sol is called the Great Animal, and Salt Armoniac is made of it; and Luna is called a Plant and

Salt Alkali is made of it, but Mercury is called the mineral Stone and common Salt is made of it. Likewise when the Philosophers saw the substance of this Art dissolved, they called it Salt Armoniac, and when it was putrefied they said our Stone was base, and is found on a dunghill, and many have dug and laboured in the dunghill and have found nothing. And when it is converted into water, then both poor and rich have it, and it is found in every place, at any time, and in every thing, although the searching aggravates the searcher. And when it was white, they called it Arsenic, and by the name of every white thing, and also Virgin's Milk, and when it was red they called it Sulphur, Jacinth and Blood, and by the name of every red thing.

Gratianus: Ashes may be made of every thing, and of those Ashes, Salt may be made, and of that Salt may water be made, and of that water is Mercury made, and of that Mercury by divers operations is Sol made.

Arnoldus: Truly this ash wants to melt, which moreover it enters favourably in order that it may tinct, melting or liquefaction is added to it, or else sweat by some means is delivered of the Philosophers. Therefore, what means is that? Is it in dissolving the waters? Surely not, because the Philosophers respect not the waters and other moistures sticking to that which is touched.

The Philosopher: Whosoever will alter and change bodies and spirits from their nature, must first reduce them to the natures of Salts and Alums, otherwise it will not be done and then it dissolveth them.

The Philosopher: Salts and Alums are those which are made in our work.

Arnold: He that hath fusible salt and incombustible oil, let him praise God.

Avicenna: If thou wilt be rich, prepare Salts until they be pure water, because Salts are converted into Spirit by fire. Salts are the root of our work.

Hermes: All Salts of what kind so ever, are contrary to our Art, except the Salt of our Lunaria.

The Philosopher: The Salt of metal dissolves Mercury in pure water, under dung and that mixture being coagulated will be a perfect medicine.

Note that, all Salts well prepared return to the nature of Salt Armoniac, and the whole secret is in common salt well prepared. Note that the Roman Vitriol hath the nature of the Stone of Metals, and it is hot and dry. Likewise, Alum seems to be coagulated Mercury, but it goeth from his accomplishment, hot and moist and it is called the like of one that is Mercury. Therefore, he that knoweth Salt and the Solution thereof, knoweth likewise the hidden secret of the Ancient wise men. Therefore, set thy mind on Salt and cogitate on nothing else, for in that only the science and greatest secret of all the Ancient Philosophers is hidden.

Conjunction or Coupling

O Luna, by means of my embracing and sweet kisses,
Thou art made beautiful, strong and mighty like as I am.

> O Sol, thou art to be preferred before all light,
> But yet thou needest me, as the cock does the hen.

Arisleus in a Vision

Join therefore thy son Gabrick, best beloved of thee among all thy sons, with his sister Beya, who is a fair, sweet and tender damsel. Gabrick is the man and Beya the woman, who gives him all that is hers.

O blessed Nature, and blessed is thy operation, because out of an imperfect thing thou makest a perfect thing. Therefore, thou must not take that nature unless pure, clean, raw, pleasant, earthy and right and if thou do otherwise it will not bring forth anything, so that no contrary thing enter in with our Stone and put nothing but that only. Join therefore our ferment with his sweet sister and they will beget a son between them, who shall not be like his parents. And although Gabrick is made more dear to Beya, yet there is no generation made without Gabrick, for the coupling of Gabrick with Beya is presently dead. For Beya ascendeth above Gabrick and includes him in her womb because nothing at all can be seen of him. And she embraceth Gabrick with so great a love that she hath conceived him wholly in his nature and divided him into inseperable parts.

Masculinus:

Conception changeth the blood, which before was as it were milk.
The pale things wax black, the red diffused things shine.
The white woman, if she be married to the red man,
presently they embrace, and embracing are coupled.
By themselves they are dissolved and by themselves they are brought together,
that they which were two, may be made as it were one body.

Mary the sister of Moses: Join Gum with Gum in true matrimony and make them like running water.

Astanus: Spirits are not joined unto bodies until they be perfectly purified, and great miracles appear in the hour of conjunction, for then the imperfect body is coloured with a firm colour with the help of the ferment. This ferment is the soul of the imperfect body, and the spirit by the help of the soul, is conjoined and knit to the body and is turned together with it into the colour of ferment, and is made one with them.

Basius: In a perfect magistery, stones do not receive themselves by course, unless either of them be first purified. For the body does not receive the spirit, nor the spirit the body, so that spiritual may be made corporeal, or corporeal spiritual, unless they be first perfectly purged from all filthiness.

O Sol, thou hast need of me, as the hen hath need of the cock, and I have need of thy work.

Alexander in the Secrets of Nature: Know that no son is born but of man and woman.

Hermes in his Second Treatise: Know this, my Son, that unless a man know how to marry and to make pregnant and to engender forms, there can be nothing done. But if he shall do this, he shall be of great dignity.

Rosinus: The secret of the art of gold consists of the man and woman, because the woman receiving the strength of the man rejoiceth because the woman is strengthened by the man.

Alphidius: Son, by the faith of the glorious God, complexion is of Complexion, between two lights, male and female, and then they embrace themselves and couple together, and a perfect light is begotten between them, which there is no light like through the whole world.

Senior: Of two waters make one water, if you understand these two words, all the Regimen will be under your feet.

Rosarius: It behoveth thee to have two waters, the one is white but the other is red. This is that water in which the powers of the whiteness and redness are gathered together.

Hali: Take a whelp dog, and a whelp bitch of Armenia, join them both together, and both these will bring forth to thee a dog whelp of an heavenly colour, and that son will preserve thee in thy house from the beginning in this world, and in another world.

Senior: The red ferment hath married a white wife, and in their conjunction the wife being great with child, hath brought forth a son which in all things hath preserved his Parents, and is more bright and glorious.

Rosinus: This Stone is a Key, for without it nothing is done. Our Stone is a most strong spirit to which bodies are not mingled, until it be dissolved, and if I should call it by its true name, the ignorant would not believe it were so.

Arnoldus: Thou that desireth to search out the secret of this Art, must of necessity know the first matter of metals, for otherwise thou shalt but spend thy labour in vain.

Rosinus: We use true nature because nature does not amend nature, unless it be into his own nature. There are three principal Stones of Philosophers. That is mineral, animal, and vegetable. A mineral Stone, a vegetable Stone, and an animal Stone, three in name but one in essence.

The Spirit is double, that is tincturing and preparing.

Albertus: The spirit preparing, dissolveth copper and extracteth it out of the body of Magnesia, and reduceth it again to its body.

Senior: It is the preparer and extractor of the Soul from its body, and bringeth it again to its body. The tincting spirit is called the Fifth Essence, which is strength and a soul standing and penetrating.

Liber Trium Verborum: It behoveth thee to extract the fifth essence, otherwise thou labourest in vain, and this without doubt cannot be done without water.

But the second Spirit is without the body and it is of a watery nature and it is a tincturing body in Elixir.

Turba: But this man is the body and this woman is the spirit.

Arnoldus: The spirit is not altered of the body so that it may lose its spiritual virtue, but every body is altered and tinctured of the spirits.

Aristotle: Note therefore the words and mark the mysteries, because the spirit which dissolves the white foliated earth, doth not hold any of them fixed, unless you possess it with that body of which it was prepared in the beginning. Permanent or Perpetual Water, or the spirit of Wine, is called the water of the body, that is when the body is reduced into Mercury. Likewise without permanent water nothing is done. It is also called Water of Life.

The Philosopher: I protest by the God of Heaven, that the Art is nothing else than to dissolve a Stone, and always to coagulate it, and again with the spirit of wine only, you may make perfect Elixir.

The Water of the Philosophers is called the Vessel of Hermes of which the Philosophers have written, "All means are made in our water - that is; Sublimation, Distillation, Solution, Calcination, Fixation, are done in this foresaid water, as it were in an artificial vessel, which is the greatest Secret". And water is the weight of wisemen, therefore, water and fire suffice thee for the whole work. Our water is stronger than fire because it makes a mere spirit of a body of gold, which fire cannot do, and fire is in respect to it as it were water in respect to our common fire. Therefore, the Philosopher says, ' Burn our copper in a most strong fire.'

Aristotle in the Regimen of Princes says unto Alexander concerning the four elements: When you have water, that is Mercury of the Air, that is of the Stone and Air of Fire, that is Spirit of Mercury and fire that is Mercury of the Earth, that is of Luna, then you shall have the Art fully.

The Philosopher: Our Stone passeth into the earth, the earth into the water, the water into the air, the air into the fire, and there is its standing. The white work is compiled of three elements, in which fire is not, that is three weights of earth, two of water and one of air. But for Elixir of Sol - put two parts of earth, three of water, and one and a half of air and of fire, and that is red ferment.

Rasis in his Great Book of Precepts: Whosoever is ignorant in the weight let him not labour in our books, because the Philosophers have concealed nothing but these things.

The Turba: Our contrition or grinding is not done with the hands, but with most strong decoction.

Calidus: A lesser fire grindeth all things.

Note, there is a difference between the element and that which is Elementated, and the Fifth Essence. The Element is the first thing of compoundable matters, from whence neither earth, nor water, nor air, nor fire is a pure element and simple with us, because they are mingled between themselves by course and especially - in that part where they conjoin. But the Fifth Essence is a body standing by itself and differing from all Elements and from things Elementated, as well in matter as in form, and as well in nature as in virtue, not having the cause of corruption in itself. And it is called the Fifth Essence, therefore, because it is extracted out of all Elementated things, wherefore there is no elemental motion in it as in other Elemental Bodies. The Stone therefore is called everything because it hath in itself and of itself every necessary thing of its own perfection. It is found in every place by reason of the participation of the Elements. It is called by all names because of the worthy and miraculous variety of colours of its nature. Most base and cheap by putrefaction, and most dear by virtue. This is the hidden and Secret Magistery of the Philosophers. Our Stone is called one thing when the substances of the body and water are prepared inseparably, so that one of them cannot be separated from another. Our Stone is said to be of a combustible matter and Mercury is only a Spirit incombustible and coppery, and therefore it is meet that it be in the magistery. Likewise, the Stone which the Philosophers seek, in which the first elements of minerals are, tincture and calx, soul and spirit with the body fixed and volatile. And it is not every Mercury, but it is that above which nature hath determined her first operations into a metallic nature, and hath left it imperfect. But if you extract this Stone from that thing in which it is found, and shall begin to work about it to perfection, by beginning in that place where nature hath left it imperfect, you shall find perfection in it and shall rejoice.

Argent vive of itself is of no force, but when it is mortified with its hidden body, then it is of force and liveth with an incorruptible life. This body is of the nature of Sol, therefore of necessity it must convert all Argent vive into the nature of Sol, as leaven converts the whole lump of dough into the nature of leaven, but not on the contrary, because always that which is ruled is transported to that which is ruling.

Our Stone is named of all the Philosophers - Mercury, which is not born as many think but extracted out of a body. The Stone of Philosophers is of three things, that is of Sol, Luna and Mercury, that is make Mercury of Sol and Luna in his essence without common Mercury, but by the philosophical way.

This Stone is but one stone in the whole world, and he that in the beginning of his work shall err from this one, doth altogether lose his labour. In the whole world there is not any other thing necessary in our work but only this Stone.

Arnoldus says Sol and Luna are in our Stone in virtue and power and in all nature, if this were not so neither Sol nor Luna would be made thereof, because the Sol and Luna in our Stone are better than the common in the nature of them, and because Sol and Luna are alone in Our Stone, and the vulgar are dead in respect of Sol and Luna.

Therefore the Philosophers have named that Stone, Sol and Luna by course, because they are in it potentially and not visibly, but in virtue and essence. Wherefore Hermes says, "Our Stone crieth saying, 'Son, help me and I will help thee.'"

Conception or Putrefaction

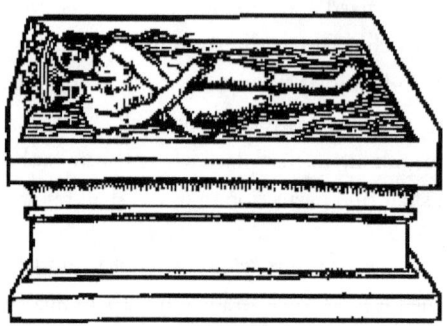

Here lie the King and Queen dead.
The Soul is separated with great grief.

Aristotle the King and Philosopher: I never saw any thing that had life to grow and increase without putrefaction, and vain would be the work of Alchemy be, unless it were putrefied.

Morienus: This earth is purified and cleansed with his water, which when it shall be cleansed, by the help of God the whole work shall be effected.

Parmenides the Philosopher: Unless the body be spoiled and putrefied and be converted into a substantial substance, then cannot that hidden virtue be extracted nor mingled with the body.

Bacchus the Philosopher: When natures are corrupted and putrefied then they engender.

Plato the Philosopher: We have an example in an egg, which first putrefies and then a chicken is engendered, which after it is wholly corrupted, it becomes a living creature.

Note, that without corruption there can no generation be made. Study therefore in putrefaction, for the corruption of the one is the generation of the other.

Hermes: The second degree is to putrefy and grind, therefore the disposition thereof is first to make it black and to putrefy it.

Plato: The first regimen of Saturn is to putrefy and to put it to Sol, but the composition is of four nights.

Democritus: Be neither too quick or too slow in putrefying the gravel and the bodies plated and joined together, attend in your work and you shall profit in it.

Rosinus to Euthiaca: Take a living creature of the Sea, dry it and putrefy it.

Morienus: No enervating nor engendering is done but after putrefaction, but if putrefaction be not, it cannot be dissolved, and if it be not dissolved it will be brought to nothing.

Morienus: Our Stone is a confection of the magistery itself and is likened in order to the creation of man, for the first thing is Coupling, the second Conception, the third Pregnation, the fourth Rising, and the fifth Nourishment.

Dear brother, understand these words of Morienus and thou shalt not err in the truth. Therefore open thy eyes and behold the sperm of the Philosophers is quick water, but the earth is the imperfect body. This earth is worthily called mother because it is the mother of all the elements, therefore when the sperm is conjoined with the earth of the imperfect body, then it is called Coupling. For then the earth of the body is dissolved into the water of sperm, and it is made one water without division.

Hali: Solution and Coagulation of the body are two things but they have one operation, because the spirit is not coagulated, but with the solution of the body; neither is the body dissolved, but with the coagulation of the spirit; and the body and soul, when they are conjoined, each of them goes unto his like. An example - when water is joined to earth, the water with his moisture and virtue endeavoureth to dissolve the earth, for it makes it more subtle than it was before, and likewise makes it like unto itself, because water is more subtle than earth. So the soul doeth the like in the body, and in the same way the water is thickened with the earth, and becometh like thickened earth, because the earth is thicker than the water, therefore there is no difference between the solution of the body and the coagulation of the spirit nor any contrary work in either if them; so that the one may be done without the other, as there is no contrary part of time between the water and the earth in their conjunction, that the one may be known or separated from the other in their conjunctions and operations. As the sperm of the man is not separated from the sperm of the woman in the hour of their coupling, and so there is one form of them, one deed, one and the self same operation at once of them both.

Merculinus:

He calleth the mixture of things
Coupling and engendering.
The seeds are mingled
As it were milk which seems to be mixed.

The second is Conception, when the earth is dissolved into black powder and begins a little to retain Mercury with him, for there the male works in the female, that is Azoth in Earth.

Aristeus: Males engender not by course, neither do females conceive, for the generation is of males and females and especially of the compound.

For nature rejoices and true generation is made by the males marrying the females, but nature being joined to a foreign foolish nature, does engender no truth of sperm.

Merculinus:

Conception, changes the blood
Which was as it were milk
The pale things wax black
And the red diffuse things shine.

Arnoldus: Every colour will appear after blackness, and where thou see thy matter to wax black, then rejoice because it is the beginning of the work.

Arnoldus: Burn our Copper in a soft fire like the hatching of eggs, until the body be made and the tincture extracted, but you must not extract it out altogether, but let it come forth all the day by little and little, until in a long time it be filled.

I am black of white, and red of white, and yellow of red, and certainly I speak the truth, and lie not. And know this, that a Crow is head of this Art, which in the darkness of the night, and in the brightness of the day flies without wings. For the colouration is taken of a bitterness which is in her throat, and redness is taken of her body, and pure water is taken of her back. Understand therefore, the gift of God and receive it and conceal it from the simple and ignorant, for it hath been concealed.

Concerning the dens and caverns of the metals, the Stone whereof is miraculous and animal, a bright colour on high mountain and and open sea. And we must confess that in the philosophical Stone after true mundification the greatest part is Argent vive and for this cause it is not burnt but by accident. But all this is done by nature, and it is not to be believed that this is possible to be done by workmanship, as diverse ignorant persons have taught. And do think for the philosophical stone is found created by Nature, and through the highest God it wants nothing more, than that may be removed which is superfluous in it. Therefore let that matter be prepared and let that which is pure be chosen out of it, and let that which is earthly be removed from it.

Tudianus: Know that our coppery and volatile stone is in his manifest cold and moist, and in his secret warm and dry. And that coldness and moistness which is in manifest, is a watery fume corrupting and making black, destroying itself and all things, and flying from the fire. And the heat and dryness, which is in secret, is warm and dry gold, and it is a most pure oil penetrative in bodies and not fugitive, because the heat and dryness of Alchemy tingeth and nothing else. Cause therefore the coldness and watery moisture, which is in manifest, to be like unto the heat and dryness, which is in secret, that they may agree together and be conjoined, and be made all in one penetrating and tincting, but it is meet those moistures be destroyed by the fire, and by the degrees of the fire, with gentle temperament and moderate digestion.

The philosophical putrefaction is nothing else but a corruption and destruction of bodies. For one form being destroyed, nature presently brings into it another form, more better and subtle. Putrefaction is the same thing that fraction of filthiness is. For by putrefaction every thing is digested, and fraction is made between that which is filthy, that which stinks, and that which is pure and clean. For a pure and clean body being putrefied doth immediately grow and increase, as is manifest in a grain of corn, which after it has stood many days under the heat of the earth, then it beginneth to swell, and that which is pure grows out of it and multiplies, but that which is filthy and naught, vanishes away. Therefore putrefaction is also necessary in our work, by reason of the aforesaid causes.

Conception and desponsation are done in rottenness in the bottom of the vessel, and the generation of things begotten shall be done in the air, that is in the head of the vessel, that is of an alembic. The body does nothing but putrefy, and cannot be putrefied but by Mercury. Putrefaction may be made with a most soft fire of dung, warm and moist, and with no other, so that nothing may ascend. Because if anything should ascend, a separation of parts would be made, which should not be done until the man and woman be perfectly joined, and one receives another. The sign is in the sight of the perfect solution, and although Azoth appears white in the first mixtion and conjunction, by reason the woman overcometh with her colour, nevertheless in putrefaction, by the benefit of the fire, they are both made black by the fire increasing in moist, it putrefies the colour black, which is tincture, and therefore to be kept a great secret.

The nature of Gold being putrefied in strong water excels all natures therefore in the making of the Stone, it is to be noted that no stone excelleth the mineral stone in virtue.

The Philosopher: Make a round circle of the Man and Woman, and draw out of it a quadrangle, and out of the quadrangle a triangle, make a round circle, and thou shalt have the Stone of the Philosophers.

Geber proves in his book of Trials that if Sol and Luna are incorporated together by Art, they will not easily be separated, and so the one converteth the other, because the one is dry and the other is moist, and after the one hath taken the other, they embrace themselves with such strong knitting and hold themselves so fast, that the one can hardly be plucked from the other. This would be much more stronger if one of them were spiritual, that is medicinal, and so tangible by reason of his spiritualness. Gold is Gold in act and in matter, but if it were spiritualised, then is made of act - power, and of matter - form and of a thing done - a thing doing, of a woman - a man, and of a thing born - a thing bearing. Therefore, since there is no matter of Gold, no Gold which was not first Silver as the Philosopher says, if therefore such a form be joined to this matter, that is to Luna, surely they will most desirously embrace themselves and make that which is the less perfect more perfect, and this is done naturally and amicably, because every nature desires to be perfect and naturally abhors to be destroyed.

Avicenna: The intention of labourers in this Art, yea rather the intention of the Art itself, according to the possibility of the nature of things, is that the matter of one thing may put on the form and nature of another thing.

Verbi Gratia: Copper is to put on the nature and form of Silver, or Lead is to put on the nature and form of Gold, and so likewise of all other metals. For since form is the nature of everything, then any thing being despoiled of his form, and another form brought to it, I doubt whether the nature of it be changed from its form. We say therefore, that the name of Alchemy in Greek signifies Transmutation and thereupon we say that Alchemy is the knowledge and science of transmuting things from their forms and shapes according to how the forms of things are divided.

The Extraction or Impregnation of the Soul

Here the Four Elements are separated,
And the Soul is most subtly severed from the Body.

Of Blackness

Hermes (in his second treatise): Know my Son, that this our Stone of many names and diverse colours is ordained and compounded of four Elements, which we must divide and cut into members and more straightly sequestrate them and mortify the parts and turn them into that nature which is in them. We must keep the water and fire dwelling in them, which is of four Elements, and we must contain those waters with his water, even if it were not water but a fiery form of true water ascending in the vessel, which contains the spirits in the bodies and makes them tingeing and permanent.

Sorin: Take of it little and little, divide the whole, grind it earnestly, until it be possessed with death of the intensity of blackness like dust. This therefore is great design, in searching out of which many men have perished, and afterwards thou shalt discern every thing separately and grind them diligently.

Hermes: We must mortify two Argent vives at once. Take the brain thereof, and grind it in most sharp vinegar or in children's urine until it be obscured. This being done it liveth in putrefaction, and the thick clouds which were upon it and in his body before he was mortified, are returned, and this being begun again as I have written it, may again be mortified as before. But we must sequestrate it from two sulphurs and decoct it continuously, till the water be made black. He therefore that maketh earth black shall come to his purpose and it shall go well with him.

Arnoldus: When the first is black we say it is the Key of the Work, because it is not done without blackness.

Speculum: Therefore my dear Son, when thou art in thy work see that in the beginning thou have black colour, and then assure thyself that thou putrefieth and proceedeth in the right way.

O blessed is nature, and blessed is thy operation, because of imperfection thou makest perfect with true putrefaction, which is black and obscure. Afterwards thou makest diverse new things to spring up, and with thy greenness thou cause divers colours to appear. That blackness is called earth, which is reiterated so often with light decoction, until the blackness remains alone, and so you have two elements. The first water by itself, and then earth of water.

Avicenna in his book of Moistures: The agent heat in a moist body doth first engender blackness, as we may see in Calx, which is made by the common sort.

Menabdes: I will that posterity makes bodies no bodies by dissolution, and to make no bodies bodies by pleasant decoction. Wherein we must take great heed that the spirit be not converted into fume and vanish away by overmuch fire.

Maria: Keep it and be careful that none of it fly into fume, and let the nature of the fire be according to the heat of the Sun in July, until the water be thickened and the earth made black, by the long decoction thereof. So therefore thou hast another element which is earth, and let it suffice thee for blackness.

Stephianus: Open thy eyes and thy heart, hearken and understand I will show and speak unto thee words that are to be understood, if thou be one of them which should understand. Know this, that from man nothing cometh forth but man, and so of every animal the like engendered, but we see some things engendered of their roots to be unlike one to another, because we see some things that have wings to be engendered of things that have no wings. We see and know also some things that we know not of what nature cometh forth, although we know it sufficeth us, but cannot give any reason for it, because they are dark and profound and perhaps hidden underneath the earth. And know that of that mineral nature the Art is made and of nothing else.

Avicenna: Know therefore the mineral root, making your work of them.

Aristotle in his second Book of the Soul: It is a most natural and perfect work to engender like to like, as a plant to engender a plant, and a goat to engender a goat.

Aristotle: The work of the Art of Alchemy would not profit in itself, unless we know the apparent natures without error.

Hermes: O, Water remaining in form, the creatress of the Royal Elements. O, Nature the chief creatress of natures, which contains Nature and meanly overcometh by Nature, which cometh with light, and is begotten with light.

Out of the Lucidary of Arnoldus

Some men have said that all the colours which may be devised in the world do appear in the work of the Stone, but that is the deceit of the Philosophers. For there appear but four principal colours, and because all the other colours draw their original out of them, therefore they called them all colours, and although all colours do not appear to thee yet care not so long as thou mayest segregate the elements. For yellowness signifies burnt choler and fire. Redness signifies blood and air. Whiteness, phlegm and water. Blackness melancholy and earth. Whereupon Hortulanus says there are four Elements, having four colours and know that the aforesaid colours appear in our dissolution.

I demand in what time this blessed Stone may be made, to which it is answered as a certain author Lelius the Philosopher witnesses, that his magistery was finished in eight days, and that another did it in seven days, and another in three months, and some in four months, and some in half a year, and some in the space of a whole year, and Maria says she did it in three days. To this I say that the cause of diversity, that is of shortness and length of time, might be defect in the virtue of the water of Mercury or because it worketh of Sol and Luna. And some of the Philosophers added more and some less. But Sol is fixed and not flying, and with that only did they work. Whereupon, for his impotency of fixion and impatiency of fire when it was mingled with Sol by melting, it caused it to ascend for a great part. And when it did ascend, so they called it water and a soul and a spirit, saying that their water was not common water nor water of Mercury. And then the earth remained in the bottom, then they reduced that water above the body and made it again to ascend by virtue of the fire, and they mingled it again with earth, until they carried out the earth with them in their belly. "The wind carried him in his belly." Therefore of necessity they must have a great quantity of the aforesaid water. And then the spirit was fixed in the body, therefore they began that subliming again until all the whole remained fixed and that which was weak ascended. Then was the spirit fixed in the body, and Luna was incorporated to Sol and commixed by the least, and so the operation was finished. Whereupon the aforesaid diversity in working might be in adding too much of the fixed body and too little of the body not fixed, and because there was not more of the unfixed body, therefore it ascended the sooner, and when there was more of the fixed then it ascended more slowly.

But what say you of this? The Philosophers say plainly, "Our Gold is not the common Gold, and our Silver not common Silver". I say that they call water Gold because it ascendeth to higher things by the virtue of the fire, and in truth that Gold is not common Gold, for the common people would not believe that it could ascend to higher matters by reason of its fixedness. Know moreover that such a manner hath been accustomed of the Philosophers, as to halt and dissemble in a most plain way, and to hide the matter that is spoken of, by figures and parables and sometimes by metaphorical words and sometimes by false and strange practise in way of similitudes.

Geber: Wheresoever we have spoken plainly, there we have spoken nothing, but where we have used riddles and figures, there we have hidden the truth.

Metrista: Salts and Alums are not the Stone but helpers of the Stone. He that hath not tasted of the Savour of the Salt shall never come to the wished ferment of ferments, for it fermenteth finitely by excellency, such is the superior as is the inferior.

Burn in water, wash in fire.
Decoct, recoct and decoct again.
Often times make moist and always coagulate.
Kill the quick and revive again and raise from the dead.
And thou shalt have truly which thou seekest,
If thou know the Regimen of the fire,
Mercury and fire are sufficient for thee.

If thou Our Copper well do know
All the other things thou mayest let go.

Out of an Ancient little book - Hortulanus upon the Epistle of Hermes:

He only that knows how to make the Philosophers Stone understandeth their words concerning the Philosophers Stone. For the Philosophers have manifestly endeavoured to make this Art known to the worthy and to conceal it from the unworthy. And so they always speak truth of the virtue of intention but not of the virtue of speech. And so they say the Philosophers Stone to be made of an egg, because there are three things in an egg, which are like to three things which make perfect the Stone. Hermes says, "Sol is its father and Luna is its mother", and thus he granteth that two things enter into the composition of the Stone, and that Hortulanus proves because the water of Sol is volatile and his body fixed, and in the contrary way with Luna. And then these words spoken by Geber and other philosophers are declared "make fixed volatile, and volatile fixed, and fixed volatile". For they persuade that there is manifest solution, because the whole work consists in Solution. Likewise when he says that it is superior and inferior, hereby superior is understood the worthier and inferior the unworthier, that one may be made of those three or that one thing may be made of Sol and Luna whose parts are equal. And this conjunction is called the Sublimation of the Philosophers, and Sublimation is called Exaltation, or Dignification, because Luna and Mercury are dignified. For when Union is made in so great dignity, then Luna is as Sol and

Mercury. Likewise when fixation is made which is called the dead body, then Sol is as base as Mercury.

Likewise, the Stone is said to have four Elements, which Arnoldus expoundeth. Because when solution is made then water is called one element, and when the body is impure, the earth is called the second element, and when the earth is calcined, it is called fire, and when the Stone is again dissolved it is called air.

Likewise the Stone is said to have body, soul and spirit. By the body we understand the impure body as was said before, by the soul is understood the ferment, and by the spirit which hath its being in projection which is called by another name, Fifth Essence, which this compostion having gotten, it has the true virtue of converting.

Likewise the aforesaid Stone is called Rebis, that is one thing which is made of two things, that is of body and spirit, or of Sol and Luna of a body purified and fermented.

Likewise it is called a Stone found in every place, because of the true composition, when Sol, Luna and Mercury are conjoined together, the virtue of the Stone is wholly through the world, in mountains and plains, that is in bodies and Mercury, and in the Sea, that is in dissolved water, and flying things take help and nourishment of it. Things flying are quick Mercury and imperfect bodies which are converted into Sol and Luna, and it is called Scorpio, that is poison, because it mortifies itself and reviveth itself again, for that threefold thing being cast upon Mercury doth revive it, because it maketh a true body and yet it is called mineral Argent vive of the Philosophers. But the matter of the Philosophers Stone is water, and it is understood of the water of these three, as Hortulanus proves, neither ought there to be more or fewer. And he says that Sol is the man and Luna the woman, and Mercury the sperm. But that there may be generation and conception, it is meet that the man be joined to the woman, and so conception and Impregnation ought to be made before fermentation, and when the matter is multiplied and fermented, then it is said that an infant increaseth in the womb of the mother. Hortulanus and Arnoldus say that the soul is poured into the body and a crowned king is born.

In the book of The Turba of the Philosophers these words are recited, "dissolve bodies and imbibe the spirit". They say bodies in the plural because there must be two, and they say spirit in the singular because it is meet there should be one. And there is no sperm without the matter of bodies unless Mercury. And when it is said, imbibe the spirit then that operation is understood which fixes Mercury and the Stone is multiplied. Multiplied, that is reiterated.

Likewise, when Mercury mortifies the matter of Sol and Luna, the matter remains like ashes, and it is called of the Philosophers searing or grinding of them. Of these ashes it is said in the book of the Turba and in the book of Arnoldus, make no small account of these ashes.

Likewise the aforesaid ashes,which is of these three things, is called by the Philosophers an impure body, because it must be decocted and calcined unto whiteness. Therefore Morienus says in the book of the Turba, "unless you purify the unclean body and make it white and send a soul into it, you have directed nothing well in this magistery". And in this sort there are two had, that is Calcination of the Stone itself and Fermentation. Calcination, that is in manner of white Ash or earth, or of white calx by the spirits, which reduction of operation is done and made with our fire, that is with water of our Mercury.

Likewise, when it is called tincture it tincteth. It is understood that if this medicine be calcined, dissolved and coagulated, it is fermented, for white is made Luna, with Sol it is made Sol.

Likewise, Geber proves and says, of the medicine of the third order, because both white and red are one and the same way with Sol and Luna, yet they differ in fermentation, of which third order this medicine is double, that is Solary and Lunary, and yet it is in one essence, and the manner of doing is one. But there is an addition of yellowness, or of yellow colour of which medicine is perfected of the substance of fixed

Sulphur. That is, either medicine is begun with Sol or Luna, for red ferment is made with Sol and white with Luna. Sol is taken two ways, one way for water of Sol, another way for the body of Sol as has been said before.

Likewise, when it is said that all colours appear, it is true, because before fermentation, in calcinations, dissolutions and fixations, all colours appear.

Light of Lights: And know that they are the same things which make both white and red, inwardly and outwardly, that is Sol, Luna, and Mercury. Which three being dissolved and fermented, he calleth them Argent vive, saying Argent vive hath in itself, Body, Soul and Spirit.

Likewise decoct the man and the woman together, till they be coagulated and made a Stone.

Likewise, you must note that Our Elixir is not made but of minerals, and note moreover, the Dragon dies not unless he be killed by his brother and sister, and not by one only but by two at once. Sol is the brother and Luna is the sister.

Lastly, Arnoldus says, because the Philosophers speak true of the Stone whatsoever they speak, because they speak of the virtue of speech to conceal it from the unworthy, but of the virtue of intention they speak to the worthy and speak a truth. And the Philosophers know that such matters ought to be declared mystically, as poetry in the manner of a fable and parable, and when the Philosophers speak of great matters, they do not mingle parables and fables, as Macrobius says.

Washing or Mundification

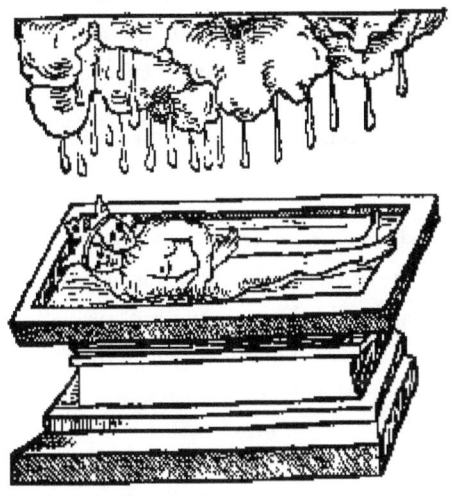

Here the dew falleth from heaven,
And washeth the black body in the sepulchre.

Senior in his Epistle of Sol and Luna: But the water which I have spoken of is a thing descending from heaven and the earth with his moisture receives it, and the water of heaven is retained and kept with the water of the earth, and the water of the earth by reason of its bondage honoureth him, and water is gathered together in water, and water retaineth water, and Albira is whitened with Astuna.

Hermes: The spirit enters not into bodies, unless the bodies be clean.

Alphidius: Take the whiteness and let the blackness alone.

Democritus: Mundify Tin with the choicest washing, and extract his blackness out of it, and also his darkness, and then his brightness will appear.

Sorin: Dissolve it with white fire until it seem like a naked sword and by whitening make the body to be white.

Rasis: Water when it is mingled with Copper doth whiten it inwardly. This whitening is called by some men, impregnation, because the earth is whitened, for the water ruling the earth increases and is multiplied, and an augmentation of a new offspring is engendered thereby.

Alphidius: Then it becomes thee to wash the black earth and to make it white without fire.

Hali: Take that which descends to the bottom of the vessel and wash it with hot fire, till the blackness thereof be taken away, and that his thickness vanish, and make the compounds of the moistures to fly from it, until there come a very white calx, in which there shall be no blot nor spot, for then is the earth able and prepared to receive the soul.

Morienus: This earth with his water is putrefied and cleansed. Which when it is cleansed, the whole magistery by the help of God shall be effected.

Hermes: Azoth and fire do wash Laton, and take the blackness from it.

The Philosopher: Make white the Laton and break the books, that your heart be not broken, for this is the composition of all the wisemen and also the third part of the whole work.

Join therefore, as it is said in the Turba, dry to moist, that is black earth with his water and decoct it till it be made white, thus you have water and earth by itself, and earth whitened with water, that whiteness is called air.

Solomon in the Seventh book of Wisdom, set down this science for light and above all beauty and health. In comparison to that precious stone, he hath not compared it, because all gold is as it were small sand, and silver is accounted as dirt in sight of that, for the getting of that is better than the work of most pure silver and gold, the fruit thereof is more precious than all the riches of this world, and all the things which are desired in the world are not able to be compared to this. The length of days and health are in his right hand, but glory and infinite riches are in his left hand, his ways are fair and laudable operations, and his bounds are moderate and not hasty but with the instances of daily labour. Wood of Life is in those which apprehend it, and a light never failing, blessed are they which possess it because the knowledge of God shall never perish, as Alphidius witnesseth saying, he that shall find this science or knowledge, his meat shall be lawful and everlasting.

Aristotle: O, how miraculous is that thing that hath all things in itself, which we seek, to which we add nothing, nor diminish nothing, but remove it only in superfluous preparation.

Arnoldus: The first matter of metals is a certain smoky substance, containing in itself an unctuous humidity or moistness, from which substance the workman separates the philosophical moistness which is fit for your work, which will be as clear as gum, in which the fifth and metallic essence dwells, and that is a gentle metal, and in it is the means of conjoining tinctures, because it hath the nature of Sulphur and the nature of Argent vive.

Geber: O how profitable is that thing, because we use that raw medicine, which after it is decocted and digested it is the greatest poison above all poisons.

Gratianus: In Alchemy there is a certain noble body which is removed from master to master, in the beginning whereof misery will be with Vinegar but in the end joy with gladness.

Astanus in the Turba: Take that black spirit not burning, and with it dissolve and divide bodies. It is all fiery and dissolving by his fieriness, dividing all bodies with his co-equals.

Rosarius: Whosoever will enter into our Rosary and there see and have roses as well as white as red, without that base thing with which our locks are locked, is likened onto a man that is desirous to go without feet, because in that base thing there is a key by which the seven metallic gates are opened, and without that base thing the precious work can never be effected. Washing is the ending of blackness, or purifying it, until white be made perfectly white, and red plain red, for Azoth and fire do take away the obscurity of the fire.

Mortification is a separation of hardness from the body, because the soul is then dead, but the body is alive by reason of the body heat and dryness. For everything that hath heat hath life and for this cause the calx of Alchemy is said to have life, because the Philosophers have studied to kill their imperfect life and to restore a perpetual life.

Reviving is by reason of nourishment, that is to say, a restoring of their perfect humour and rectified moisture by the expedition of that imperfect moisture.

Out of a certain torn paper

Now I make manifest unto thee by natural knowledge the Secret Stone of the Philosophers which is decked with a three fold garment, the Stone of Riches, the Stone of Charity, and the Stone of Curing all languishing. And in it is contained every Secret, and it is called the Divine Mystery given of God, and in the world there is not a more higher thing, after a rational soul. You must diligently note, I have told you that our Stone is decked with a threefold garment, that is, divided into three parts, into a body, a soul, and a spirit, whereupon the dead body which wanteth a spirit is dark and misty.

If thou wilt, my Son, that the body be revived, then put his soul to it again, and it will live presently.
0, Master, I understand it not.

My Son, I will tell it thee more plainly. One Stone or one thing only, because the body is reduced into its nature, that is into its water, that is into its first matter, because the first matter of bodies is an unctuous and slimy water. Then it is first called one thing when the substance of the body and the water of Union are inseparably united by the least parts, and the Philosophical Stone, of which infinite branches are multiplied, and this is called the known Stone in the books of the

Philosophers. Therefore, my Son, from that Stone is its own proper water extracted, and in the spirit by manner of separation. Sublimation which we use is an elevation of unfixed parts but the unfixed parts are elevated by fume and wind.

But we will that those two be fixed together and yield gentle fusion or melting, and so understand our true and certain sublimation, and the stone which no man can touch with his tongue. Hermes says, "Divide the subtle from the gross". Let the earth be calcined and the water sublimed. The earth remains downwards the water ascends upwards. The earth is purged by calcination, the water by sublimation, and both by putrefaction. The water defends the earth that it burns not, the water is bound by the earth that it fly not, and they both being sufficiently purged are made one inseperable, because one without the other cannot be. One part thereof being cast upon an hundred parts of Argent vive, doth tinct it into true silver, and if it shall be such tincture, one part of it being turned into red, doth tinct as many parts into true gold, of which gold there can be no better found, and this is of hidden nature and gotten by the heat of the fire.

Note, the spirit of the Lord was carried upon the waters before the creation of heaven and earth. Genesis first chapter.

We may see therefore that all things are created of water. God divided this water when he spoke, and commanded part of the water to go into the dry land, and called it earth. And He preserved the unconverted water for the earth to be dew and moisten it, because dry earth yields not much fruit, unless it be oftentimes wetted with rain water, and without rain water it seldom or never bears fruit.

Of the Rejoicing or Springing or Sublimation of the Soul.

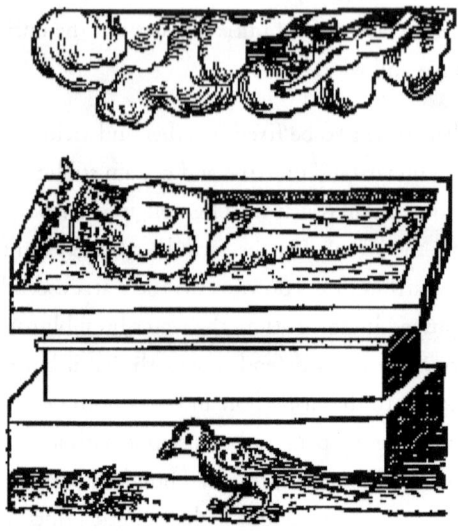

Here the Soul descendeth from on high,
And revives the putrefied body.

Now follows the fourth word and it is that the water, which shall be thickened and coagulated with the earth, may ascend by sublimation. Thus you have earth, water and air. And this it is which the Philosophers say make it white and sublime it quickly with fire, until the spirit go out of it, which you will find in it, and it is called Avis or the Ashes of Hermes.

Morienus: Make no small account of the Ashes, for it is the jewel of thy heart.

Turba: Augment the regimen of the fire, because after whiteness it comes to ashiness, which is called calcined earth, which is of a fiery nature.

Morienus: The calcined earth remains in the bottom, and is of a fiery nature, and so you have four elements in the aforesaid proportions — dissolved water, whitened earth, sublimed air, and calcined fire.

Of these four elements, Aristotle speaks in his book of the regimen of principles, "when you have water of air, and air of fire, and fire of earth, then you have the full art of philosophy", and this is the end of the first composition, as Morienus says patience and delay are necessary in our magistery, surely hastiness is partly of the Devil in this magistery.

Hermes: A dead thing will be revived and a sick thing be healed. It behoveth thee to join the body and the soul together by contrition in Sol.

Hermes: Sow your gold in white foliated earth.

Senior: Let the upper fume descend to the lower, and fume conceives from fume. This divine water is a King descending from heaven. It is the reducer of the soul into his body, which revives after his death, and life is by it and afterwards death shall not be.

Rosinus: For the body rejoices when the soul entreth into it, but the body possesses the soul, and every that hath found out the soul doth easily possess it, and note this, that the soul is punished with the body and is imprisoned with it, and by it is turned into a body.

Hermes: The spirit is the extracter and reducer of the soul and the reformer of the whole work, and all things which we seek are in it. Nothing more base in sight than that, and nothing more precious in nature than that, and God hath not ordained it to be sold for a price.

Hermes: It behoveth us to have the knowledge of the beginning as well of natural things as of artificial things, for he that knoweth not the beginning, cannot come to a good and perfect end. This secret is the life of everything and it is a water, and water takes in hand the nourishment of man and of other things, and in water is the greatest secret. But that you may not err, it is convenient for you to know that our sublimation is nothing else but to exalt bodies, that is to bring them into a spirit, which is not done but with gentle fire. For we say thus, he is sublimed into a Bishop, that is exalted. And therefore, common sublimation, which is only effect, that is to say, that the body now to be sublimed is made so spiritual, that it may be sublimed. It belongeth nothing to our work, neither is it any more required after the preparation of the first stone, because such sublimation doth not make spiritual, but only shows the effect of spirituality.

Geber: In the work of our magistery we need but one vessel, one furnace and one disposition. This you must understand after the preparation of the first stone.

Genesis: Of water all things are made and the spirit of the Lord was carried on the water, and the beginning of the generation of man was of water.

Hermes: O strong nature, overcoming natures and causing natures to rejoice.

Geber: It is convenient not to be ignorant of the chief principles and roots of this Art, which are of the essence of the work.

Basius: Our sulphur is stronger than any fire.

Alanus: There is one thing to be chosen of all things, which is of a black and blue colour, having a metallic and liquid form. And it is a thing hot and moist, watery and burning, and it is a living oil, and a living tincture, a mineral stone and a water of life of wonderful efficacy.

Aristotle: No tincting poison is engendered without Sol and his shadow, that is his wife.

Sublimation is of two sorts. The first is the reviving of the superfluity, that the pure parts may remain separated from the elemental faeces, so that they may possess the virtue of the fifth essence, and this sublimation is the reduction of bodies into a spirit, when as the corporeal thickness passes into the thinness of the spirit.

The second sublimation is extraction, because it is in it, of the nature of the fifth essence separated from the elemental faeces. But I call the fifth essence a tincting spirit wherein washing is necessary, that the unctuousness of Arsenic, or the oily nature of the purest unctuousness, which bound by his faeces, may be extracted by it, which faeces suffer it not to be sublimed.

Vincentius of the Stone of the Elixir
Vincentius in the natural looking glass in his first book: The alchemists have endeavoured in mineral bodies like the work of nature to do that in a short time, which nature does in 1000 years. Whereupon they have taught to do a certain thing, which transmuteth those bodies on which it is cast, and this they call Elixir. And it is called a Stone and no stone. A stone because it is grinded. No stone, because it is melted and runs without evaporation as gold. Neither is there any other thing with which that propriety may agree.

Avicenna: Therefore Elixir is a thing which is projected upon a greater body and changes the thing from its nature into another nature, but it is done when the lesser body and the spirit and the elements and the ferment are mingled, and there is one confection made of all of them. And Elixir is a Greek word, which sounds [like] a great treasure, or the best of treasures. And truly the Elixir, which mingles itself with the body, is as Tutty with Copper, but the Copper is enervated or grows from that Tutty, the reason for which that Tutty is an earthly thing, but Elixir is a spiritual thing, and by the nature of its kind, returned to another kind.

The Alchemist: The Elixir is made two ways, one way out of mineral spirits and clean prepared bodies. Another way out of certain things coming from animate things, as out of hair, an egg, or blood.

In the first way thus, the spirits are mortified and sublimed, until they are made clean. After this, one of the generated bodies by nature is burnt until it may be grinded, then it is calcined until it is made clean after the manner of a calx.

But at length the spirits and bodies so prepared are grinded and imbibed with the sharp distilled waters. Afterwards they are so long inhumidated, until they are turned into clear water, then they are congealed, at the last they are put so long in the fire, until they are made fixed.

Of the Complement of the Elixir

Avicenna in his epistle to Rases: The Elixir therefore tingeth with his tincture, is drowned with his oil, and fixed with his calx, and the white is completed with three things, in which there is not fire, but the Citrine or Yellow is completed with four whole things.

The Gloss: True it is that the White Elixir does not want but three things, that is to say, Oil, Tincture and Calx, but the Red needs four, that is to say Oil, Calx, Tincture, and Tincture again which is called fire, and therefore Avicenna adds, "in which there is not fire ".

Of the Manifold Fire

But the fire is manifold, and the quality of it diverse, distinguished by certain degrees, for some fire is hot in the first degree, and moist in the second degree, that is to say of horse dung, the property of which is that it does not destroy the oil, but increases it by its moistness, for others destroy it by reason of their dryness. To this fire, therefore, there is not likened any other fire in the world, unless it be the material fire of the body of a sound man. But the fire of the Sun is hot in the same degree, but it is dry. This is that which tames the thing, and is made of the animated thing, and is nourished as a boy to whom milk is given in the beginning, for the boy is nourished and increased out of hot and moist. So the fire of the horse dung increases the oil with its humidity, but it fastens the stone by its heat being temperated.

There is another fire between these two which is hot and dry in the second degree, as the fire of a furnace after bread is taken out. This melts gently and does not burn, because there is not a flame in it nor the strength of heat, for the heat in declining by little and little goes back. But if it should stand it would fix the spirit in the body, or without the body. But the fire of the horse dung, neither melts nor burns, but tames and increases the moistness.

There is a fourth fire of the furnace of the fixing, this melts and fixes, but it does not burn because it is not flammable, nor differs from the foregoing, unless it be in that there is a continual heat, which is not in the foregoing.

The fifth fire is flaming, and it is hot and dry in the third degree. This only calcines and does not melt, that is, for the making of gold and silver, and of other bodies, in the same degree or further. And it is a fire in the furnace of calcination.

The sixth is hot and dry in the fourth degree, and this melts and fixes strongly by mollifying the bodies sweetly. Neither does it separate or disperse them. This is fire of the furnace of melting in the same degree.

The seventh fire is a fire of leaves which dissipates and disperses and melts bodies.

The eighth is that which melts and calcines, and it is flaming because flame only has his operation in it. Coals and flames is the substance of fire, and in that flame only of wood. This is also in the same degree with the fires going before.

The ninth also is in the same degree, that is, which is master to them all, as the fire of office, that is of trial. This melts and burns, and dissipates and disperses that which is bad, it saves and rectifies that which is good, it is as it were a judge discerning the good from the bad.

The Fire of Juniper

Continual Artificial fire lasting in what degree you will have it, by the space of one, two or three months, until the coals be bare, therefore you must always keep them covered, and you may augment or diminish your heat according to your pleasure, and that is according to the addition of more or less kindled coals.

First, see that you have sufficient store of ashes, made only of the wood of Juniper, then have a great earthen vial, and in the midst thereof, let there be another glass or crucible, and put in the ashes and set the great vial over the heat of the fire, until the ashes wax hot and so surround the lesser vial, and set coals made only of wood of the aforementioned Juniper upon those ashes, and you must have more hot ashes of the same wood, which you must sprinkle on the aforesaid coals, and cover them with their ashes made very hot, and have you matter to be put into that lesser pot or glass, and put a cover on the greater glass and set it on a stone under a bench or on a bench but upon a stone, lest by some chance misfortune happen to it. By such practise you may prepare many such fires. You may likewise put hot water into the lesser glass, or the moist belly of the horse, and into it the vial of the matter.

You shall make the aforesaid coals in this manner. Cut wood of Juniper into small pieces of the thickness of two fingers or more, put them into a great pot well stopped and luted on every side, and filled up to the top. Set that pot, the space of one whole day, over a strong fire of a furnace of wind or flame of wood, and let it cool by itself. Then open the glass, and that you shall have that you desire, but you must burn the ashes after the common order. This fire may be fire of the first or second degree of fixing of spirits.

Here is born a noble and rich Queen
Whom the wisemen liken unto their daughter
She increaseth and bringeth forth infinite children
Which is immortal pure and without spot
The Queen hates death and poverty
She excels both Silver and Gold and precious stones
And all medicines both precious and base
There is nothing in this world like unto her
For which we render thanks to Immortal God

Luna speaks:
Violence oppresses me being a naked woman
For before my body was as it were outcast
Neither was I yet a mother, until I was again born
Then I got strength of all herbs and roots
I have obtained victory in all diseases
I was the name of my Son
And being joined with him, I came forth with him
And being great of child by him
I have brought forth an unripe fruit
I am made a mother and yet I am a virgin
And in my essence am so constituted
That my son should become my father
According as God hath ordained it essentially

Sol:
My mother which brought me forth
Is again brought into the world by me
There is one thing to be considered, that is natural copulation
Which lieth hid artificially in the mountains
Where of four things are made one thing
In our artificial stone
And six things are considered threefold
And are brought into one substance

He which understandeth those things well
It is granted unto him by God to expel all diseases
Whatsoever both in metals and also in the bodies of men
But no man can do it without the help of the Deity
From my earth there springs a fountain
From which two rivers come forth
The one holds his course towards the East
The other towards the West
From whence two Eagles flying burn their feathers
And being bare and naked fall again to the earth
These Eagles are presently renewed with fair feathers
And both Sol and Luna are subject to them

0 Lord Jesus Christ
From whom all goodness proceeds
By the grace of thy Holy Spirit
Which protecteth all things,
We are made to understand the sayings of the wise men
That we may consider and provide for the life to come
When our bodies and souls shall be conjoined again.

Hermes: Know, you searchers after rumours, and you children of wisdom that the vulture being on the top of the mountain, crieth with a great voice saying, "I am white, black and red, the yellow or citrine. I am a speaker of the truth and no liar."

Alphidius: Argent vive, which is extracted from that black body, is moist, white and pure, that it perishes not in the outward.

Morienus: It is convenient for thee to know that white fume is the soul and the spirit of these dissolved bodies, and surely if the white fume were not, the gold of the white stone could not be.

Rosarius: This is our most notable Mercury, and God never created a more excellent thing under heaven, the Soul only excepted.

Plato: This is our matter and our secret

Hortulanus: Thus you have two Mercuries extracted from those two bodies, and it is well washed and digested. And I swear by the ever Living God that there is no other Mercury in the universal way, than that which hath now been declared, on which all philosophy dependeth, he that says otherwise says falsely.

Parmenides in the Turba: Some men hearing water named of the Philosophers, think it to be the water of a cloud, but if they had any reason, they might know it to be permanent water, which cannot be permanent water without its body with which it is dissolved.

Alphidius: The Philosophers have called that medicine by all names because there are so many names given unto this Mercury, that there can very hardly be any more titles attributed unto it.

Plato: We have revealed all things, the secret of the Art only excepted, which may not lawfully be revealed to any man, but we attribute that to the glorious God, who inspires whom He will with it, and conceals it from whom he pleases.

King Solomon: This is the daughter, for whom the Queen of the East is said to have come from the East, rising in the morning to hear and to understand, and to see the wisdom of Solomon. And there is given in her hand power, honour, and virtue, a flourishing crown on her head with the beams of the seven shining stars, as she were a bride adorned with her man, having written in her garments with golden letters, in the Greek, Barbaric and Latin tongue, "I am the only daughter of the wise men, and altogether unknown to the foolish".

Hermes: As Sol in the stars, so Gold in metals. Sol gives light to the stars and contains all fruit. The day is the nativity of the Light and Sol also is the Light of the day, which God hath created for our use, that is for the Government of the world. Tincture ought to be corporeal and extracted from perfect metallic bodies, by the benefit and means of the minerals.

General Rules

The First Rule
Everything is of that into which it is dissolved. For as ice is converted into water by means of the heat, therefore of necessity it must be water before it be ice. So all metals have first been argent vive, which is manifest, because when they melt in the fire, they are converted into it. Note here that the Philosophers calleth a liquid metal Mercury or Argent vive, therefore the reduction of metals into Argent vive in this sort is called that melting, although it may be done by violence of the fire. But because in that strong liquefaction it retain the form of Argent vive, therefore he nameth it Argent vive, but that is not the philosophical solution but that of the layman.

The Second Rule
Every nature desires naturally to be finished and abhors to be destroyed, and flies away. Therefore nature embraces that greedily which is agreeable with her, and as much as she can, refuses that which is contrary to her. And according to that, Art ought to imitate nature, for otherwise it always errs.

The Third Rule
Every worse thing labouring in any art, does of his own natural malice endeavour to destroy that which is better. Every better thing labouring in any art, endeavours to make perfect that which is worse. Therefore, first of all thou must know the natures of things, that you may discern what is better and what is worse for nature, and where it may be perfected and where hindered, and that the quality of the worse exceed not the quality of the better, for otherwise you shall err greatly.

The Fourth Rule
Everything that is dry does naturally desire to drink his moisture, that it may be continuated in his parts. Here note, what is the radical moisture

of all melting things, and feed with such moisture the overdried, and it will be made temperate, and thus you shall have your desire.

Out of a certain approved little treatise concerning the difference of common Sulphur, and simple Sulphur of the Philosophers not burning.

When as the Philosopher says generally that Sulphur coagulates we must say that it does not, because every common sulphur, according to the Philosopher, is strange and contrary to metals.

Avicenna says that, that enters not into the magistery which is not sprung from it, because it always infects and makes black and corrupts however it be prepared by workmanship. For it is an infection of the fire and therefore hinders the melting, but if it be calcined it goes into an earthy substance, like dead powder. How can it therefore inspire life into another thing, for it hath a double superfluity that is, an unflammable substance and an earthy feculency. Therefore consider by those things, that common Sulphur is not the Sulphur of the Philosophers, when as the Sulphur of Philosophers is a simple, quick fire, reviving other dead bodies and ripening them, so that it supplies the defect of nature, when, as it is of a superfluous ripeness according to that which is perfect in nature, and by workmanship is more and more purified.

Whereupon Avicenna says, such Sulphur is not found on the earth, but as much as is in these bodies Sol and Luna, and that is in another thing which is told unto no man, unless it be revealed by God himself. In Sol it is more perfect because it is more digested and decocted. For the Philosophers have subtly imagined how those sulphurs might be chosen in those more perfect bodies, and to purge their qualities by Art, that they might have this art by the help of nature which has not appeared in them before, although they have first had it fully and secretly. And they grant that this cannot be done without the dissolving of the body and reduction of it into his first matter, which is Argent vive of which they are made from the beginning, and that without any mixture of foreign things. Which foreign things do no way perfect our Stone, because there is nothing convenient for it but that which is by affinity near unto it, when, as it is a medicine of a virtuous and simple nature, drawn out of Mercury water, in which gold and silver are first dissolved. For instance, if ice be put into simple water, it is dissolved in it by heat, and returns into its first watery substance, and so water is tincted even by a secret virtue which was in the ice, but if ice be not resolved into water by heat, it is not joined to the water, but lies in the water; neither does it tinct the water by its virtue, which before was coagulated in it. So in the same way, if you resolve not the body into Mercury, with Mercury, you cannot have the secret virtue from it, that is Sulphur digested and decocted into minerals by the work of nature. For so it is one Stone, one Medicine, which according to the Philosophers is called Rebis, of a twofold thing, that is, of a body and a spirit, white and red, in which many of the ignorant have erred.

How Sulphur is red in Sol, and white in Luna

Whereas it is said that the Sulphur of the Philosophers is red in Sol by greater digestion, and Sulphur, white in Luna, by lesser digestion. Whereupon the Philosopher says Citrination is no other thing than completed digestion, for heat going into moisture, first engenders blackness, and going into dryness causes whiteness, because the fire if it transcends the agent in it changes it into a most pure citrineness. All these things may be done in the calcining of lead. And the Philosopher says that now in act everyone of the perfect bodies contains his good Sulphur with Mercury, that is golden gold and silvery silver. Therefore white Sulphur by citrine is Gold, where the Sulphur in it is red Sulphur, the substance of the fire, which has more digested this white, and so Sulphur white and red of either part is in Sol. Wherefore the fire is its perfection, and in fire it is engendered, and therefore it rejoices friendly with the nature of its fiery nature.

Whereupon no foreign thing can cause this in bodies, when as art is nothing else by the help of nature, but a decoction and digestion of that nature by simple labour. For instance, in the morning when I rise and see my urine white, I judge that I have slept but a little, then I lay myself down again to sleep, and after I have slept, my urine is citrinated, and by this reason of a greater digestion of natural heat being in me. So follow nature by art, in like sort to decoct it, to digest it, to ripen it, and to sublime it, seeing that nature in act contains in itself a natural fire with which it is ripened. Those things have not this and therefore they cannot give it. In Luna there is nothing but white Sulphur, simple, but not digested like red, nor so purged from blackness by the working of heat, which it contains naturally in itself, but the form of fire is covered and hidden, working more in art than in nature. And therefore it is not impossible, that Art may do it by the help of nature, but by itself it cannot be, unless it be moved by art and operation. But those labours (as I think), come not to a man of an hard brain, and therefore true Gold is not made unless it be so digested and decocted, that the better may better the worse, because the intent of all the Philosophers is to effect it with the better, which the ignorant sort understand contrarily, because they endeavour to bring to pass the better with the worse, and this they seek in a thing which never was in it, that Gold and Silver in adustible things as hath been before explained.

That it is not profitable to seek this Sulphur in some sick bodies because it is not there.
It may worthily be demanded, whether this white and red Sulphur to tinct Mercury, may be chosen out of some sick bodies. I say that it cannot, because it has been before said, that there is not any thing of a greater temporancy, than is found in these two bodies, in which the tincting beams are. Whereas it has been said that sick bodies contain in themselves stinking and adustible Sulphur, and not of a virtuous nature as in those. Whereas every art is not of force, but by what nature had before, from which it follows, you may purge metals by the lesser minerals. Which being purged yet they should not have that golden and silvery nature in themselves, because golden digestion and decoction have not been in them as in others, nor Sulphur so ripe. And therefore we must help these which be unripe with those that are ripe, that they may be ripened. Therefore they tinct not but they are tincted, because

the tinctures of gold and silver have a proportionable nature with them, that is with the unripe and the imperfect, because they have drawn their original from Mercury. By this it manifestly appears that the lesser minerals cannot tinct, because the imperfect metallic bodies, which agree not with Gold or Silver of the part of ripe Mercury, cannot tinct nor receive the nature of Gold or Silver, and therefore is not to be tincted, but in those, in which the virtue of tincting is tincted therefore with Gold and Silver, because Gold gives a golden colour and nature and Silver a silvery colour and nature. Wherefore neglect all other things which have not naturally the virtue of tincting, as there is no fruit in them, but only destruction of things and gnashing of teeth.

Fermentation

Here Sol is again included,
And is circumpassed with the Mercury of Philosophers.

Hermes in his Second Treatise of Sol: O Sons, there are seven bodies of Philosophers of which their gold is the chief, the king and head, which neither the earth corrupts, nor any burning thing burns, nor water alters, because his complexion is temperate and his nature direct in heat, cold, moisture and dryness. Neither is there anything in it that is superfluous, nor any thing too little. Wherefore, the Philosophers have brought it forth and magnified it, and they have said that Gold is in the same sort in bodies, as Sol in the stars with his glorious light and shining, for by it vegetables spring in the earth and all fruit is brought forth by the will of God. In like sort, gold in bodies contains every body with itself and receives them, because it is the ferment of the Elixir, without which nothing is done. For as dough without a leaven cannot be leavened nor seasoned, so when you will make white, sublime, mundify and extract the faeces and filthiness from them, and [you] will make them fit, conjoin and mingle them together, then put ferment to them, and look in what sort the ferment of dough is, so in the same sort is this ferment. Meditate therefore, and contemplate whether the ferment be of the thing or else of its nature. This is the key of all the Philosophers, and we must note that ferment whitens confection, forbids combustion, and holds tincture that it flies not away, it softens bodies and makes them enter by course and conjoins them.

Raimund says in his Apertory: Now by the second part the Stone will colour itself, it is fixed and fermented, but the ferment of the stone for white is Silver, and for red it is Gold, as the Philosophers declare, because without ferment neither Sol nor Luna cometh, nor anything else that is of his nature. Join, therefore, ferment with his sulphur, that it may engender its colour, and likewise come to its nature, weight, sound and savour, because every like engendereth its like, and ferment tincteth as Sol and changeth his Sulphur into a permanent and penetrating medicine. Therefore the Philosopher says, he that knows to tinct Sulphur and Argent vive, attaineth the greatest secret, for this cause it is meet that Sol and Luna be in the tincture and the ferment of that spirit, and of the permanent water of Argent vive. And by that water these natures ought to be fixed and nourished with natural heat until they shall have fixation and melting perfect. After this is made the Regimen of the Conjunction of the Stone with its ferment, that is until the work is come to its full accomplishment and this is not done at one time all together, because this is not of the intent of nature but to have it well by coupling, that is a little, and then a little again, and also by coagulation the true unformal medicine is made. And for this, that copulation is caused of the subtle parts transmuted and altered into a spiritual form and essence, because it is written that the thick and gross body with the subtle, and the subtle with the thick and gross, cannot conjoin themselves by reason of their contrariety, unless that which is gross be converted into his subtleness by his subtle spirit, and then they are to be mingled together. And this the Philosophers notify by declaring to a follower of the truth, and they say that perfect mixture is the union of mingled and altered bodies joined to themselves by things not to be divided, because these things are here required by manifest reason. Because mixture or union cannot be done or made without alteration which is subtlization of the body and reduction of it into spiritual form.

And concerning that part the Philosophers do say that now the medicine is finished from one manner into another crystalline manner, and then it will appear, because that plate is without division of those parts, by little and little. For that, such a cause cannot be done or made without the subtlization and homogeneity of nature, and for this cause it is meet that this matter may become so subtle, that all parts in nature may be equally mixed with water. And, this you may see by your understanding, when one body is made transparent and continuated into one by conjunction or commixtion of many parts without division, discontinuation and termination, into one thickness and transparent figure throughout all its parts.

Now, my Son, thou hast no small secret. Therefore, first illuminate the body before thou put the soul into it, because otherwise it will never receive it or retain the spirit in it. Thus for Raimund.

Calidus: No man yet ever could, and hereafter never shall tinct foliated earth but with gold, therefore Hermes teaches us saying, sow your gold into white foliated earth, which by calcination is made fiery, subtle and airy.

Therefore let us sow gold into that earth, when we put tincture of gold to it, but gold can never tinct any other body perfectly than itself. Surely this cannot be done unless it be brought to pass by art.

Gold is the ferment of the work without which nothing is done, because it is as the leaven of dough, the curd of milk in cheese and as musk in good sweet things, and with it the composition of the greater Elixir is made, because it doth illustrate and preserve from burning, which is a sign of perfection. Know that without gold the work cannot be done, nor amended, because gold is the headstall of Argent vive and none congeals Argent vive unless in the body of magnesia, in which there is one burning thing, and another a flying thing, and the gold itself is the third thing receiving the tinctures of them and is the tincture of redness, and Argent vive transforms every body with it. From whence a certain man said, unless you put gold in gold you do nothing.

Aristeus: Know most assuredly that if a little gold be put in the composition there will go forth an open white tincture - by the ferment of Sol is understood the sperm of the man, by the ferment of Luna, the sperm of the woman. Out of them is first made the coition. Afterwards is made a true and chaste generation. The ferment of gold is gold, as the ferment of bread is bread.

Rosarius: As in the work of bread, a little leaven lightens and leavens a great plenty flour, and so that little of the earth which this stone contains, does suffice for the nourishment of the white stone.

Of the double difference of Minerals - Out of the same little tract

But mineral bodies are specially distinguished into two parts. That is to say, into a metallic part and a mineral part. Into a metallic part, that is, into metals which draw their original from Mercury, and into a mineral part which does not come from Mercury. An example from metals - Sol, Luna, Jupiter, and Mars has its mixture of gold and silver. An example from minerals - Salts, Inks, Alums, Arsenic, Auripigment. All metals are ductile and liquefiable which draw their original from Mercury, because the matter of them, out of a watery substance mixed with an earthy substance, by a strong commixtion that the one cannot be separated from the other, wherefore that watery substance is congealed with cold more after the action of heat and therefore they will be more fabrile or ductile, and the water only is not congealed but only with the earthly dryness which alters the wateryness, when as there is no unctuous moisture in them, because the congealing of them is of earthly dryness. Therefore they are not easily dissolved unless by the vehement action of the heat in them, according to which they are most easily commixt. But there are lesser and and middle minerals which take not their original from Mercury, and of these are Salts which easily melt in moisture, as Alum, simple Salt, Salt Armonick, stony Salt and all kinds of salts. And surely they have virtue in them. Neither do they easily melt with moisture only, as Auripigmentum, Arsenic and Sulphur, when as the wateryness of sulphurous bodies is mixed with slimy earth, by strong commixtion, with the fervency of heat, until they be made virtuous and then they are coagulated of cold. But Inks are compounded of salts, sulphur and stones, and it is thought that a mineral strength of certain liquid bodies is in them, which they are made of, as Calcanthum and Olocari. But metallic bodies cannot artificially be made of them, when as they are of another nature, and with metals being of the first near nature, that is they take their original with Mercury, that is of Argent vive. I deny not, but that metals may be purged and dissolved with them, only a sophistical form be brought into them to deceive men.

There are two sorts of sulphur, that is, living and burning. That which is living causes metals, although they yet differ one from another, the second because it is more infected with the sliminess of the earth, when as simple living sulphur causing gold and silver, is nothing but a vapour hot and dry, engendered of the most pure terrestrial dryness, in which the fire bears all the sway, and that is called an element with the Mercury of metals.

That it is impossible for the lesser metals to be made artificially.
But because in the chapter going before it hath been determined that it

is impossible the lesser minerals are to be made metals, therefore here it remains first to be proved in this way. Because the lesser metals are engendered of the first matter of metals, which is Mercury, because the generation of them differ in the first with the generation of Mercury, in form, in nature and in composition and therefore cannot be made metals, because it is one first matter and sperm of one form of things, of which they are engendered. The first part of that which went before is manifest, that the lesser minerals are not engendered of Mercury, because they continually remain in the first matter of metals.

Whereupon Aristotle and Avicenna say, therefore if they should be made metals, then it is meet that first they pass into the first matter of metals. But because this cannot be done artificially, therefore metals cannot be made of them. Thus far hath the first part of that which went before, been sufficiently declared. Secondly to the same, that the lesser minerals cannot artificially be made the beginning of metals which is Mercury. Therefore, also they do not thoroughly come into the middle and end, which are metals and tincture, which it holdeth, because nourishment in man, by generation cannot be made man, unless it be first converted into sperm, and so being added to his like, a new man is engendered. But because the lesser metals are of a foreign nature from metals, although they participate well in some mineral force, and are of a weaker virtue and combustible, therefore, metallic nature rejoice not in it, but resolves and preserves those things which are of its nature. For instance, if water be mingled with earth it is separated by course, because the earth requires a bottom, for it is heavy and dry, the water requires the upper part and cannot so artificially be conjoined, that those contrary natures should stand jointly in one nature. The water can well wash and purify the earth, but it ought not to be believed that the dryness of the earth can be changed into a watery moisture, although the earth becomes moist by the water, so surely the lesser minerals may be conjoined with metals and purge them and by some means bring in a new form into them, but nature granteth not them to remain with them, and to make that ripe which is unripe. Wherefore the ignorant bring in divers sophistical matters to deceive men, that is unproportionate things which neither yield matter nor also receive it, as the privates of men, the eyes of animals, eggshells, hairs, the blood of a red headed man, worms, herbs, roots, and man's dung. For many of the ignorant sort have laboured and do yet labour in these vegetable and sensible things, where they have found out no truth, but certain humilities which we will declare to the ignorant that they may avoid the deceits. For they have extracted a long time out of these things, afterwards to be spoken of, which they call artificial Argent vive and oils and waters, which they named the four elements, namely water, earth, air, and fire, and Salt Armonick, Arsenic, Sulphur and Auripigmentum, which they could have bought cheaper in the market and had sooner brought it to pass. They have sought also in vegetable and sensible things, where they have found out no truths, of dry things wanting moisture, of combustible and corruptible things in which they have sought tincture, which they have not, but those are damned by apparent loss. And these are the matters - man's hair, the brain, man's spittle, the milk of women, man's blood, urine, man's dung, menstruum and sperm, the bones of dead men, hen's eggs, and simply in all brute beasts, in fishes, flying creature, in worms, scorpions, toads, natural and artificial Basilisks, in which very great trumpery is, in shells and in the juice of certain herbs, flowers and trees, and especially in those, that is the herb of Lunary, and Solary, which is called Toxicum, and in all things of which they have feigned names at their pleasure concerning the metals, deceiving themselves and others who were desirous to do the best matters with the worse things, and to finish the defect of nature with such like things whereupon it is said "whatsoever a man soweth that he shall reap", if therefore he shall sow dung, he shall reap dung, wherefore it is no marvel that scarce one among a thousand or no such men at all, bring it to pass. Sow gold and silver, and it will bring unto thee most pleasant fruit by thy labour with the help of nature, because that only hath the thing which thou seek, and no other thing of the world, whereas all other things are stinking and give place to nature by the continuance and trial of the fire. And there are other Alchemists labouring in lesser minerals, that is to say in four Spirits as in common Sulphur, Arsenic, Auripigmentum, and Salt Ammoniac being desirous to make a tincture but this they cannot do as is manifest by the definition of the tincture. For to tinct is nothing else than by tincting to transfer that which is tincted into its own nature, and to remain with it, without any transformation, and nature teaching nature to fight against the fire, for the nature of the tincting and the tincted agree. For instance, if you tinct Lead or Tin, or any such thing from gold or silver, this agrees in natures, because both parties have taken their original from Mercury. The ripe is conjoined with the unripe, that the unripe may be effected by it in such a way.

But since these four spirits are of another nature from metals, as has been sufficiently spoken of, therefore, if they must be tincted, I demand whether they ought to change or to be changed. If to be changed then it is not tincture, as is manifest by the definition thereof. If to change, therefore, in tincting it converts into its nature that which is earthly and strange to a metallic nature. Therefore, they cannot make metal by tincting, but that, which in tincting it converts into its nature, is tried, because everything engendering, engenders his like, and because this tincture is an earthly generation of four spirits, therefore it will engender a thing like unto itself, which is also earthly as itself.

Illumination

Here Sol plainly dies again,
And is drowned with the Mercury of the Philosophers.

Therefore regard not that tincture, nor any other which is not found in the property of nature with all foreign ways, because in them there is nothing else but the consuming of things, the loss of time and labour, whereas all other things are apparent, and not being metals, which are laboured by the lesser minerals and such like.

Raymund: Although this our stone does now naturally contain tincture in itself, for it is created perfectly into the body of Magnesia, but of itself it has no motion unless it be brought to pass by art and operation. Geber says in the operation of roots, "operation is used for this, that the tincture of gold may be bettered more in gold than it is in its nature, and also that it may be made Elixir, compounded according to the Allegory of the Wisemen". But whether we need gold only and not any other body. Harken unto Hermes speaking "His Father of the first composition is Sol, and his mother is Luna". The father is hot and dry engendering tincture, his mother is cold and moist, nourishing that which is engendered. Therefore if there were not one of them in our stone the medicine would never melt easily, nor gain any tincture, and if it did give, yet it would not tinct, but in as much as it were, Mercury would vanish away in a fume, because the receptacle of the tincture should not be in it. But it is our final secret to have a medicine that melts or flows before the flight of Mercury. Therefore the conjunction of two things is necessary in our work. For Geber says in his Perfect Magistery, gold is the most precious of metals, for that is a soul conjoining the spirit with the body, that is with the imperfect, because as the body of a man without a soul is dead and unmoveable, so an impure body without ferment, which is its soul, is earthly and vegetable for that is the tincture of redness, transforming every body. It is ferment converting the whole mass or lump to its nature, because as Sol and Luna overrule all the other planets, so those two bodies have dominion over other bodies of metals, which are strongly converted to the nature of the two aforesaid bodies. And therefore, it is called Ferment for without it things springing cannot be amended, and as a little leaven corrupts a great lump of dough, that is, transmutes and seasons it, so in the same way, it happens to our stone.

Hermes: My Son, extract his shadow from the sun beam. Take therefore the fourth part of it, that is one part of the ferment, and three parts of the Imperfect body, dissolve the ferment in his equal quantity of water of Mercury, decoct it also with a most soft fire and coagulate the ferment, that it may be made as the imperfect body, and the mouth of the vessel being stopped, in the same manner and order as has been said, it is prepared in all points.

Aristotle: Choose to thyself, a stone by which Kings are honoured in their diamonds, and by which Physicians have to cure their patients because it is near the fire.

My Son, take of the most simple and round, and do not take of the triangle or quadrangle, but of the round body, because the round is nearer to simplicity than the triangle. We must note therefore, the simple body having no corner, because it is the first and last in planets, as Sol in the stars, because we see in Astronomy of the firmament, that Sol is the Lord of all Planets, and all Planets have need of his light because he gives light upwards even unto Saturn, and downwards even unto Luna, and then he behold all, both superior and inferior.

Aristotle: My Son, thou ought to take of the fatter flesh. Thou ought to know that every seed answers his springing, because those things which you sow, these shall you reap again.

What things are particular which are brought to pass in this art

I declare universally to all men, to whom these my present speeches shall come, that in the bound of the whole art, there are but two particular things which are particularly brought to pass according to philosophers and nature. The first particular, as well in white as in red, is in Mercury or in the administration of the perfect medicine, although the body doth secretly contain in itself the tincture of it, with which it is brought to pass as nature requires, because that is particularly in it of either form of things. When as Mercury is compounded of the first matter of all metals, of white earth too much sulphurous, and of clear water. And therefore, the whiteness of the earth engenders the clearness of the water and there is a most white colour in it, as experience teaches us, and it contains in it good sulphur, perfect and pure. Then it is possible that Sol and Luna be made of it particularly.

The Philosopher: Let it be mingled with workmanship with other metallic bodies because it is of the nature of them and they are engendered of it and therefore it may be done by workmanship, and let it imitate the digested nature into it, that it may be affected with them, so is made like unto them without any foreign commixtion, when as it rejoices simply in the nature of its nature, and not by any foreign thing. But, with Sol Sol is made, Luna with Luna, Venus with Venus and so with all the rest. When as every thing sendeth his strength into it and also because it contains his good sulphur, but imperfect, which by art is made perfect wherefore other metals coagulated by Sulphur particularly adjustible [burning], as it cannot be made Sol and Luna.

The first reason: for if they should be transformed into Mercury and should be mixed with Sol and Luna, then the Mercury of them would have in itself that bad Sulphur, and if it should be purged then it would not be purged into so much, which should reduce it into Mercury as before such simplicity, neither also could the body be dissolved into it by Mercury and when it cannot be dissolved then also it cannot send his serated strength into it.

But natures being serated or ingrafted of each part, every one is separated from the other in trial, when it has not secretly in itself a perfect nature with which they might effect it by the solution of them, but it is always necessary for them, by the help of Art, that other perfect bodies should succour them, with their nature which naturally is perfect.

Secondly, if the imperfect bodies should be adjusted to the perfect bodies, Silver and Gold could not be made, when as naturally the natures of them are locked in either part by congelation, and when there is no mean opening, those natures to send one strength into another, then they cannot be joined by natural conjunction, so that they may return into Mercury from whence on each part they took their original. And therefore by the vehemency of the fire they are separated by course, by combustion of imperfect nature, as is well seen. But when you will conjoin them, make Mercury by Mercury, which dissolves and opens locked natures, that simply one may pass into another, and the perfect send strength into the imperfect, that it may be made perfect with it, and these are the labours of the particular way, and so Gold and Silver may be made particularly.

Note that raw Mercury dissolves bodies and reduces them into their first matter and nature, but the Mercury of bodies cannot do this. That is because of the rawness of its Sulphur, which it had in the first white earth, with which it is made from the beginning of clear water, because that [which is] raw does always desire to gnaw that which is nearest its nature, first Gold, secondly Silver, etc., but the other Mercury congealed of bodies cannot do this, because by congelation that raw sulphur, which before was in it, is altered in nature, therefore it gnaws not as the first, nor opens that which is locked. And therefore, one strength is not sent into another, but everything remains by itself, whereby surely they are fluctuously joined, but are naturally locked in each part.

Wherefore, by the trial and sharpness of the fire, the imperfect is burnt, the perfect remaining, because one nature cannot help another, but this way do it with crude Argent vive, that is to lock and open natures that every near thing may be in aid to its nature. Therefore if Silver be dissolved, he shall find a silvery nature, if Gold, a golden nature, if Lead, a leaden nature. It is congealed by their Sulphur. Whereupon the Philosopher says, "But if those bodies, which participate their nature, as you seek in many stinking and unclean things and therefore it is particularly possible on either part, for Gold and Silver to be made of it, and not in other bodies as you hear."

Note that there is a double solution of bodies into Mercury by Mercury and into Water of Mercury. The first solution is required for particular things, the second for universal things.

The first solution of bodies into Mercury is but a resolution, that is, that which is locked by resolution only, and opened for the entrance of one nature into another, and that is resolution in particulars.

The second solution is into water of Mercury and it is done universally, and that is not done only by dissolution of unripe Sulphur into Mercury, but by putrefaction of the body and spirit into moisture, when as putrefaction is the solution and separation of all natures bound by course, and so the parts bound are separated every one part from another. And this is done by the separation and solution of the elements, which in the generation of Mercury are connected, that is, of water and earth and those parts while they are purged are joined in nature by conversion, and loose themselves more for their cleanness than before in nature, and this separation cannot be in bodies but by a spirit. So art transcends nature in one way, although artificial things may well be done suddenly, which naturally before took longer.

Do not believe that these are common elements, that is to say, cloud water and such like, but cold and dry earth, cold and moist water, moist and hot air, hot and dry fire, and so are the Elements in Nature. But art cannot so separate the connected parts in generation that they should be simply transmuted into those elements, which they were, when as the first nature has changed one quickly into another. In such way the Art may well be separated, as moist from dry, and cold from hot but yet one quality of the natural commixtion possesses the nature of the other in some part, by those things with the help of art, they might be joined, as they are divided. If that were not that one quality should participate in the nature of another, that is, water participates in the nature of earth in coldness, and air in the nature of water in moistness, and so in all the rest, then it would follow that the natural work would be wholly destroyed, when as the elements should be be most simple, as they were before. Before the generation of Mercury Art had destroyed nature, beginning from the head, that is from Gold and Silver, even to the beginning that is Argent Vive and beyond those principles of simple elements, according to that which they have been before the generation of Mercury, so that it is impossible in Art. If it were possible then it would follow that Art would make Elements afresh, beyond the first matter of metals, and would again engender Mercury as it destroyed it, which is impossible to be done artificially. Surely Art is well destroyed from the head even unto the feet, that is, edificating Mercury from the feet even unto the head in a more subtle form with the substances of nature, which before was Art. So the forms of things are divided, when as they are transmuted into another form than that which they had been before. As Aristotle says, "Let the Artificers of Alchemy know, that the forms of things cannot be transmuted which is true unless they be reduced or converted into their first matter, that is into Argent Vive, otherwise it is impossible to be done."

Nourishment

Here Sol is made black like unto pitch,
With the Mercury of the Philosophers.

The second particular is in Sol, Mercury, and in the Sulphur of the Philosophers

Whereas it has been before said, that Luna contains white Sulphur in it, as Gold does red, yet the form of fire is hidden in it under the whiteness. Therefore it is possible for all Silver to be made Gold. Whereupon the Philosopher says, "It is not Gold unless it has first been made Silver." So Silver contains in itself certain undigested qualities, which may be purged from it by Art, so that particularly it passes into fixed Mercury, and into the nearest nature of Gold, because it then contains everything in itself that Gold contains, by the apposition of the red Sulphur of Philosophers, with which it is more digested, and the citriness in it is caused in the joining of the perfect body, when as they are simple of one nature. But this is impossible to be done in other bodies, as they have not so great vicinity or nearness to perfect nature, as that which is our impediment in the engendering of them, by adustible and stinking Sulphur. Neither are they of Mercury, of which the Philosopher speaks, "It cannot pass from the last to the last, but by the middle." That is, Gold is not engendered of Mercury unless it be first Silver, neither has it in itself Sulphur of the simple fire, not burning, but burning Sulphur and therefore they cannot particularly be transformed into fixed Mercury, as has been said before by Aristotle.

Let the Artificer know that they may make things like to them, and tinct by red citrine, that it may seem to be Gold, and tinct white with white until it be much like Silver. They may also take away the uncleanness of Lead or of other sick bodies, that they may seem to be Gold and Silver, but yet Lead always remains Lead, because it has not in it the digested qualities of Gold and Silver. As those which take Salt Armoniack or other lesser minerals to delude men, and join Copper or Tin with Mercury, so that it may appear to men to be Silver, and malleable in some sort, and are able to endure the trial in the fire. According to them which are skilful in the fire, which nevertheless are deceived in this, because it has not in it the silvery nature, as appeareth in the colour and trial.

The first reason is, Copper contains in it Mercury, somewhat clean, in as much as there is of Sulphur, but the Sulphur is stinking and adustible, which burns it and has redness not well digested, but by reason of the red and unclean Sulphur. While the Mercury has the substance before the Sulphur, and therefore it goes more slowly in the fire, than Lead or Tin, because Mercury resists not, but in as much as it suffers violence of the Sulphur mixed with it, but that Lead is sooner burnt, that is by reason of the infected Mercury. But infected Mercury with infected Sulphur, is as Lead, seeks some moistness of its imperfection, and when Silver and Copper are mingled in Silver it finds not any thing but an infected thing. But in Copper it first finds burning Silver, to which it is sooner mingled, and in the universal mixing, the Mercury is more infected with Copper, when as Lead is infected in either part, that is of Mercury and Sulphur.

And now, because more evil does sooner cleave to evil, so much the more weak and worse it will be, and therefore sooner sticks to Copper and Silver, infecting and burning it with the nature of Copper and Silver as you have heard. On either part it is locked and cannot help the worse, and so Lead burns the Copper from the Silver, which is more slowly separated without Lead, because how much the more imperfect it is, so much the more weak and combustible it will be. But in the conjunction with Copper and Mercury, by some means it opens the natures and conjoins these two, that is, Tin and Copper. Tin has clean Mercury and bad Sulphur, weakly mixed, Mercury is joined with Mercury. And Mercury hath always the power of Sulphur, by changing the colour of Copper which is in Sulphur, so that a new form may appear, and may not also quickly burn the Sulphur as it did before that Mercury. And when crude Mercury is coagulated by it, it is altered with them in nature, as by some means it may appear to be Silver, although in truth it be not Silver. When as due digestion and decoction shall not be in it, and Sulphur, not of a simple fire, and of a virtuous nature, as Argent Vive itself, of which Gold and Silver on either part, that is of Mercury and Sulphur, are sufficiently digested and of good ripeness, and perfect in all digestion.

Thus you have the sophistical Silver of Copper, Tin and Mercury, and then if you mingle some powders of the lesser minerals, it is not impossible if Mercury has the government, but yet always when it is imperfect, it is in the end diminished and burnt in the fire, when, as the Sulphur is not of a virtual nature as the Mercury, but always secretly hurtful and infecting the Mercury, although the Mercury be well furnished, and so in the end it returns into dung, as it was before. Understand, therefore, how the true Gold and Silver differ from the sophistical, although many sophistications are made by the same manner by other metals into red and white, adjoined with the lesser minerals or with some one of them. But those labourers are deluded, when they think themselves to have found the good appearance, their ignorance is the cause of this, because they know not the natures of metals.

Fixation

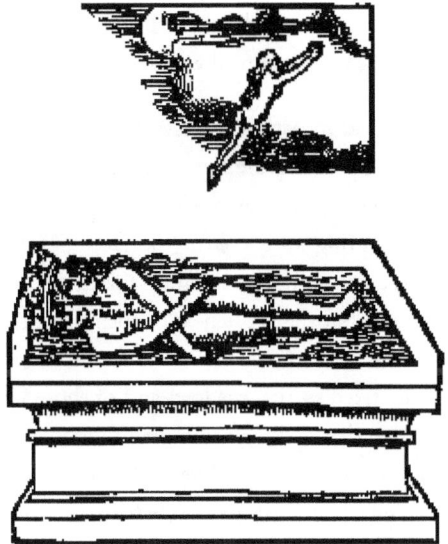

Here ends the life of Luna,
And the spirit subtly ascends on high.

Raymund: Now I will speak of fixation of tincture, or of Copper which carries tincture in it, and which is done by calcination of which way I will stop.

Lelius the Philosopher: In the end a king shall come forth unto thee crowned with a precious crown, shining like Sol, glistening in brightness like unto a carbuncle, melting like wax, persevering and abiding in the fire, penetrating and retaining Argent vive.

Arnoldus: For the colour of redness is created of the accomplishment of digestion, because blood is not engendered in man, unless it first be diligently decocted in the liver. So we, in the morning, when we see our urine to be white, then we know we have slept but a little and we go to bed again, but after we have received more sleep, then the digestion is accomplished and our urine is citrinated. So by decoction only, whiteness may come to redness by continuing the fire in that way, and our white Copper, if it be diligently decocted may be made perfect red. Let it therefore be decocted with a dry fire and with dry calcination, until it wax red like cinnabar, and put neither water nor any other thing into it, until it become decocted to the accomplishment of the red.

What yields Fusion and Ingestion and also Fixation
Geber in the Second book and the first Chapter: We say, because the perfection of every solution is drawn with subtle waters, especially sharp and bitter, and with spring waters having no faeces, as distilled vinegar is, and sharp grapes, sour pears, and pomegranates distilled in like sort, and such like as these, but the subtleness of them has been the cause of the invention thereof, which have neither fusion nor ingression of which a great profit of the fixed spirits was lost, and of those which are of nature, for everything that is dissolved must of necessity have the nature of Salt or of Alum, or of some such like as this. But it is the nature of them because they give fusion or melting before their vitrification, therefore the dissolved spirits will in like sort yield like fusion. Seeing therefore they much agree with themselves in their nature and bodies it is needful to penetrate bodies by it, and in transmuting to penetrate and in penetrating to transmute, but it comes not to this without the magistery, which is that after the solution and coagulation. Thereof some one of the spirits, purified and not fixed, should be administered to it and so often sublimed in it until it remains with it, and yields it a more speedy fusion or melting, and preserves it in melting from vitrification, for it is the nature of spirits and bodies not to be vitrified and to keep the mixed from vitrification until the spirits shall be in it. Therefore, the more we preserve the nature of the spirit, so much the more we defend it from vitrification. Therefore, by the work of nature we may prove that the grounds of Salts and Alums, and of such like, preserving nature to be dissolvable, for we find not in all the works of it any other thing to be dissolved besides these. Therefore, whatsoever things are dissolved, must of necessity be dissolved by the nature of them, by the reiteration of calcination and solution. Therefore, we prove it by the fact that all things calcined are near to the nature of Salts or Alums and therefore must of necessity accompany themselves in

the propriety. But the manner of Solution is of two sorts, that is, by hot dung and by hot water, of which there is one intention and one effect. The manner thereof by dung, is to put it into an earthen body and to pour upon it a quantity of distilled Vinegar, or such like, and to stop the head thereof close, that it breathe not out, and to set it in warm dung, three days, and afterwards let that which is dissolved be removed by distillation of a philtre, but let not the dissolved be calcined again, until by reiteration of the work it be dissolved upon all that. But the order which is done by the boiling of the water, is more speedy, and it is as calcined into a body. It is in like sort ordered with Vinegar, and the hole is stopped that it fume not out, and it must be buried in a cauldron full of water and straw, as in the manner of distillation by water we have taken a precept by order, and afterwards let fire be kindled underneath it, until it boil the space of an hour, but after this let the dissolved be distilled. The melting in the middle fire by which the Ingestion is made, is the last of perfections. As Geber says, in his Seventh Book chapter 17, "Let all resolved things be coagulated by the help only of the fire, and that in the vessel strongly stopped, and keep this secret of mine, because the thing is perfectly coagulated, if not, then begin the work again, and by reiteration you shall come to your work again, by the help of God."

Raymund: Our infant has two fathers and two mothers, and because it is charily nourished of the whole substance in the fire, therefore it never dies. Ceration is the reducing of moisture above the earthy by the help of the fire, that by calcination it being deprived of moisture and being made dry like sand, it may be mollified and reduced to melting, and in consequence may have ingression, but not by common liquefaction which the common people melt by fire, but by a philosophical solution which is done by water.

Fixation is when the body receives the tincting spirit and takes away his volatileness, and it is done by often iteration, until it be made ashes of perpetual enduring, and that the whole remain in the fire.

How of Mercury metals especially are engendered

The nature of all melting things is of Argent Vive and of the substance of it, because Argent Vive is proper to them, because it is coagulated of vapour or of the heat of white or red Sulphur not burning. Whereupon Aristotle says in his first book, "If it be white Sulphur not burning, it congeals Mercury into good Silver, but if the Sulphur shall be pure with clear redness, and if the fever of the fieriness simply not burning shall be in it, it congeals into most pure Gold, better than the mineral has brought forth." Because every dry thing does naturally suck up his moisture, that it may be continuated in his parts, therefore the vapour of the Sulphur of Argent vive is to be coagulated of a subtle, earthy substance, decocted and undigested, from the first commixtion, united unto it in the action of heat, afterwards elevated, decocted and digested, until it has a sulphurous strength of coagulating Argent vive into metallic bodies. Gold has much of the virtue of Sulphur and but a little of the substance thereof, and much of the substance of Mercury and little of the virtue thereof. Which by reason of the Mercury it is very heavy and by reason of the Sulphurous virtue it is very red. Silver in all points is in a contrary manner, because it has much of the substance of Sulphur and but little of the virtue thereof, and little of the substance of Mercury and much of the virtue thereof. Therefore, it is white, because colour follows the multitude of virtue, but virtue is placed in vapour, his matter is nearer the matter of Gold, than any other metal, therefore it is more easily turned into Gold. It needs no other labour but in transmuting the colour and giving the weight.

The Difference of Oil and Water in the Manner of Tincture

Arnoldus: There is a difference between the tincture of water and oil, because water does only wash and cleanse, but oil tinges and colours. As for example, if cloth be drowned in water, it is cleansed by it and when it is dried the water goes away and the cloth remains in its state and in that colour which it had before, but that it is more clean. And it is contrary to this in oil, because if cloth be dipped in it, it is not separated from it, by the heat of the fire, or of the air, unless that be wholly destroyed, neither can the oil be separated from that cloth, but by washing and by the dryness of the fire. But water is a spirit extracting the soul from bodies, and when the soul is extracted from those bodies, then it remains born in that spirit as the tincture of things tinged is carried by the water upon the cloth, and then the water goes away by dryness, and the tincture remains fixed in the cloth by his oilyness. So therefore, water is a spirit in which the tincture of the air is carried, which when it is brought upon the white foliated earth, presently the spiritual water is dried up and the soul remains in the body, which is the tincture of the air. Therefore, the spirit retains the soul, as the soul retains the body, because the soul stays not in the body, but by the help of the spirit. But when they are conjoined they are never separated, because the spirit retains the soul as the soul retains the earth. Whereupon Hermes teaches us that souls are to be honoured in stones, for their mansion is in them. But there are retainers of fugitives with them. Therefore it is our coagulation, because they retain it flying. Sow, therefore, the soul into the white foliated earth because that retains it. Because when it would ascend from the earth into heaven and would descend again into the earth, it will receive the strength of the inferior and superior.

Of Inceration, or the Manner of Reducing Water upon Earth

Arnoldus says, therefore, pour in water by grinding by courses and afterwards by calcining it gently, until that water shall suck up the fiftieth part of his water, knowing that first the earth must be nourished with a little water and after wards with more, as is seen in the education of an infant. Therefore grind much by imbibing the earth, by little and little with water from 8 days to 8 days, decoct it in dung, because by the inward moistening, the burning is taken away and the thing is brought into his first matter, and afterward calcine it meanly in the fire, and let it not be irksome unto thee to reiterate it oftentimes, because the earth brings not forth fruit without much labour and ploughing, and if the trituration shall not be good, till the water may be made one with the earth, the body brings forth nothing. Therefore, withhold not thy hand from the trouble of grinding and drying, because it makes the earth white, but take heed that you imbibe not the earth but by little and little, supply it with long grinding, after the drying of the earth, then there is a weight in this everywhere to be noted, that is lest overmuch dryness or superfluous humour corrupt it in administering. That is, that you may decoct so much by drying as the Dissolution has added to it, and dissolve it by imbibing as much as by drying it is lacking. Therefore pour water over it temperately every time after the calcination, neither too much nor too little, because if it should be much, it would be made the sea of calcination, and if too little then it is burnt into ashes or dross.

Wherefore, work your earth gently and not over hastily, from 8 days to 8 days, decoct it in dung and calcine it, until it shall imbibe the fiftieth part of the water in it. And know that after the imbibing, it must be moistened inwardly the space of 7 days, therefore begin the work again many times, although it be long, because you shall not see the tincture until it be accomplished. Study, therefore, when you shall be in every work, to record all signs which appear in every decoction and search out the causes of them, and bear them continually in your mind.

There are three colours, black white, and citrine, when the earth goes forth the blackness is imperfect.

Therefore, every time little by little strengthen the fire in calcination, until the earth come forth white by the strength of the fire, for as heat working in moisture gives blackness, so working in dryness yields whiteness, therefore, if the earth be not white, grind it with water and afterwards calcine it again, because Azoth and fire wash Laton, and do take the obscurity from it. For his preparation is always made with water, therefore, what the clear water is, such is the clear earth, and how much the more the earth shall be washed, so much the more white it is. Therefore, by the manifold reiteration of Imbibing with strong grinding and often drying of the wateriness of Mercury, the greater part is consumed, that is of the wateriness, the residue whereof is in like sort revived by the reiteration of Sublimation. These words Arnoldus uses in his Rosary, word for word.

Of the Manner of Subliming and making White, and a Recapitulation of the Whole Magistery

But when the earth shall draw out the fiftieth part of it from the water, then sublime it presently with as strong water as you can until it ascend upward in manner of most white powder. But when you shall see the earth like pure white snow in whiteness, and as dead powder to stick to the brims and sides, then reiterate Sublimation upon it again without the faeces remaining beneath, because, part of that being fixed does stick and would be fixed with the faeces, and can never be separated from them by any kind of policy.

But the powder ascending upwards from the faeces is ashes extracted from ashes, and earth sublimed and honoured, but that which remains beneath is ashes of ashes, and the lower ashes is to be condemned and disposed as faeces and dross. Make, therefore, a difference between the clear and bright thereof, because when it is most white and ascends like snow then it will be accomplished. Gather it, therefore, warily that it fly not away in fume, because it is a good thing to be sought for, a white foliated earth, congealing that which is to be congealed and cleansing that which is to be cleansed, and purifying Arsenic and white Sulphur, of which Aristotle says that it is the best thing the Alchemists can take, that of it they may make Silver.

No man ought to sublime earth for the works of sophisters but ought to sublime it for the perfect Elixir, and those which are sublimed are sublimed in two manners, or by themselves because they are spirits, or with others because they incorporate in themselves with the spirits. For Mercury when it is a spirit is sublimed by itself, but our earth when it is calx is not sublimed unless it incorporates itself with Mercury. Convert therefore the calx and imbibe Mercury and decoct it until it be made one body and let it not be tedious to thee to reiterate it oftentimes because the body will not ascend upward unless it be incorporated with Mercury. Therefore it is needful that you subtilate its nature as much as you can and strongly decoct it with Mercury until it be made one, because we make not Sublimation but that the bodies may be brought to a subtle nature and matter, that is that they may be spirits and that the body may be light, to govern in every thing, either in Sol or Luna, and this sublimation we make in order that we may bring bodies into their first nature and matter, that is into Mercury and Sulphur. Therefore we make this Sublimation for three reasons. Firstly, that the body may be a spirit of a subtle matter and nature; secondly, is that Mercury may incorporate himself with the calx; and thirdly, that the whole may take the white and red colour. Therefore when calx is sublimed to Luna it ought to be white and Mercury likewise white, and Calx when it is sublimed to Sol ought to be red and Mercury ought in like sort to be red, being made hot with the fire and it ought to be an incerated powder.

Put not the red Mercury to the white nor the white unto the red, but place every form with his own form and put it to the fire being hindled and sublime the whole and mingle not that which remains down below. After you shall begin again to sublime by the incorporation of Mercury until the whole shall ascend, otherwise do not put it into the magistery. Let the Alembic wherein you put the Mercury be glazed and let the cucurbit be of glazed earth, and let the mouth of the bottom be large that the Mercury may ascend up more freely, but the Alembic must be joined with the cucurbit so that the Mercury may not fly forth or evaporate away, lest the Magistery perish.

Multiplication

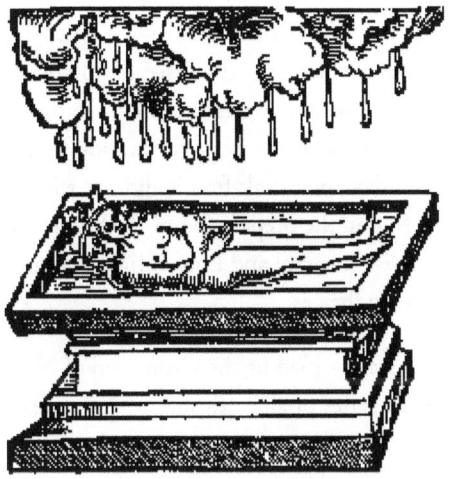

Here the water is diminished,
And bedeweth the earth with his moisture.

The Seventy-Ninth Chapter of the Third Book of Geber

The additional amount of sulphur not burning perfectly administered is made for the preparation of the medicine of Sol with the industry of subtilty by means of fixing and calcining and by the manifold means of Solution with much reiteration until it be made clean. Surely perfect administration goes before these things which is effected by sublimation and it is of this sort, that is the manner of additament by reiteration of the part of the sublimation of the unfixed stone, with the policy of conjoining until it be elevated with it and again be fixed with it that it stand. And when the order of the exuberance of this accomplishment is reiterated oftentimes and the medicine is multiplied more, the goodness of it is more augmented and the great perfection is multiplied.

And we to avoid the taunts of the impious will declare the whole accomplishment of this magistery under short speech are completed and known. And the intention thereof is that the stone may be most perfectly cleansed by means of the sublimation, and the addition of it.

And surely from hence, that which is volatile may be fixed of them by the means of policies, but from hence that which is fixed may be made volatile, and again the volatile fixed, and in this order the most precious secret is accomplished which exceeds all secrets of sciences of this world, and it is an incomparable treasure, and then by great diligence and labour, and continuance of earnest meditation thou may be raised up into it, for with that thou shalt find it and not without it and by diligence he may find in the preparation of the Stone, that it will transmute Argent vive into Sol and Luna infinitely more pure and perfect than naturally they are.

And now blessed and glorified be the Great God of Natures who hath revealed unto us the series of all medicines with the experiences of it which by the goodness of his investigation and by the instances of our labour we have gotten and we have seen it with our eyes and touched it with our hands and although we have concealed it under dark speeches. Yet let not the children of Learning marvel at it, for we have not concealed it from them, but we have delivered it to the improbate and the wicked under such dark speeches, for that it is necessary so to do, yet the wise and virtuous may by diligence attain unto it. Therefore, you Sons of Learning seek after it diligently, for this most excellent gift of God is kept for you only. You ignorant men and Sons of impiety and of wickedness, fly from this science because it is an enemy unto you and will bring you into the miserable state of penury, because by the divine judgement and providence this gift of God is utterly hidden from you, and altogether denied you. Thus for the words of Geber.

Geber in his First Book and 26th Chapter: We grant therefore unto thee according to the opinion of the ancient men which were following this art, that the natural principles of the work of nature, are a stinking spirit, that is Sulphur, and quick water, which we also grant to be named dry water. But we have divided the stinking spirit, for it is white in secret and both red and black in the magistery of this work, but in manifest both of them tend to be red.

Geber in his Second Book Chapter 39: The consideration of things helping perfection is the consideration of the natures of those things which we see sticks to bodies without workmanship and to make a mutation as Marchasites, Magnesia, Thusia, Antimony and the Lapis Lazuli, and the consideration of those things which with sticking or cleaning, cleanse the bodies such as Salt or Alum, Satpeter and Borax and such things as are of its nature. And what is the consideration of vitrification, cleansing by the like nature.

The Cleansing of most sharp Vinegar according to Geber in his book of the Investigation of this Magistery
Vinegar of what kind soever it may be made subtle and purified, and his virtue and effect by distillation may be bettered. We have spoken sufficiently of the cleansing and purifying those things with which imperfect bodies may be prepared and purified and be made more better and subtle by a due fire always helping it, for they are prepared and purged by them by the intention of the fire in this manner, for these imperfect bodies have superfluous moistures and a burning sulphuriness and a blackness ingendering in them and corrupting those aforesaid bodies. For they have an unclean earthiness, stinking and combustible, very gross and hindering impression and melting. These and such like things are in these foresaid bodies which are to be found in them by our experiences and politic investigations. And because these superfluous things happened accidentally in these bodies and not radically therefore the spoiling of those accidental things is possible, therefore it behoves us to take away all superfluous accidents with artificial fire from these aforesaid things, the substance only Argent vive and of radical Sulphur remaining. And this is the full preparation of the imperfect things and the perfect depuration cleansing, bettering and subtilisation of these things or of this pure substance remaining is done many ways, according to which the Elixir of preparation does want. Therefore this is the manner of depuration in general. For first of all the superfluous moisture is to be elevated with a proportionate fire and corrupt in the essence of them and also the subtle and burning superfluidity. And this must be done by calcining, then all the

substances remaining corrupt in the calx of the superfluous burning moistness and blackness of them, is to be gnawn away with those aforesaid clean sharp or bitter corrosives, until the calx shall be white or red or coloured clean according to the body, the nature and property, and pure from all superfluity and corruption. And these things are cleansed with those corrosives by grinding, imbibing or washing, but afterwards all the unclean earthiness is to be taken away and also the gross and corruptible stinkingness with the aforesaid things clean and pure nor having metallic fusion or melting purified with the aforesaid calx in the aforesaid manner, commixed and well grinded, which in the melting or reduction of the calx will retain within themselves the gross and unclean earthliness, the body remaining pure and cleansed from all corrupting superfluousness.

The ordering of the subtilation and bettering of the pure substance of those things in general is this. First, this purged and redacted body is again to be calcined with the fire and with the help of the aforesaid cleansing things, and then is to be dissolved with these things which are solutives, for this water being our Stone is Argent vive of Argent vive and Sulphur of Sulphur, extracted, subtilated and attenuated of a spiritual body which may be bettered by strengthening elemental virtues into it with other preparatives, which are made of the kind of its kind and by augmenting its colour, fixion, weight, purity, fusion and all other things which appertain to perfect Elixir.

And this is the way found out by us alone, of preparation, depuration, subtilisation, and melioration of mineral bodies in general.

The Multiplication of the Elixir is made in two ways. The one is done by reiterated solution and coagulation of the Stone. The second by projection of the first Stone of Elixir upon the body either white or red in such quantity that the same body may also be converted into the medicine and let this be put together to dissolve in their water and menstruum, and thus the first Elixir is ferment of such tincture and thus the woman bakers do.

Of the Inceration of the White Elixir

Extract it therefore from hence from a crystalline plate which you shall find clear in the bottom and first grind it and cerate it with the last inceration, by dropping upon it drop after drop in a crucible upon a gentle fire of his white air until it be melted like wax without fume. Then try it upon a fiery plate. If it resolve itself speedily like wax then it is cerated, but if not then take and cerate it again drop after drop of his white oil, until it be melted like wax without fume. And surely this is the precept of all the Philosophers, that when you fix the sublimed part into the most clean part of the earth, that then you would reiterate the sublimation of the other part not fixed, upon that which is fixed, until that also be fixed. Try this upon the fire and if it give good melting then you have sufficiently reiterated the sublimation, but if not then reiterate the Sublimation of the unfixed part upon that, until it be quickly melted like wax without fume, then extract it and suffer it to cool.

And now in the aforesaid chapter note diligently the zealous intention of the Author in it how often he reiterates the manner of inceration. It might have been sufficient to have repeated it but once, but because he might the more strongly and deeply imprint it into the understanding of the reader, therefore he repeats it so often, because in it the whole strength of the Elixir depends. Consider also that Ceration, Fixation and Sublimation are all one and their acts are alike, for by inceration the spirit is fixed and the body is sublimed.

Arnoldus in the previous chapter: Keep the water 7 times distilled because it is the solvative Mercury of the Philosophers, making matrimony and Aqua Vita washing Laton. And as you have done with the white water so shall you also with the red water because they have one and the same manner of washing and a like effect, but that only white water is to make white and red water is to make red. Therefore mingle not the one with the other because you shall err in so doing.

Arnoldus in another chapter: But if it melt more hardly, which is the defect of ceration, then help it with oil, that is with air by dropping drop to drop upon a light fire, until it melt like wax, and when you incerate it then mingle more of the hot and moist thing than of the cold and dry. And when you fix it then mingle more of the cold and dry things than of the hot and moist. Therefore understand what I speak because the permutation of nature is the perfection of this work. Note of the aforesaid things, that water, air and oil are all one, that is Spirit of mineral Mercury.

Arnoldus in another Chapter: The principal manners of the Regimen are four. That is to dissolve, to wash, to reduce, and to fix. To dissolve the gross into simple and to make it subtle, to wash the obscure into bright, to reduce the moist into dry, to fix the volatile upon a fixed body. To dissolve is to divide bodies and to make the matter or first nature. To wash is to inhumate, to distil and to calcine. To reduce is to impregnate, to incerate and to impregnate, and to subtilate. To fix is to resolve, conjoin and to coagulate. By the first the nature is changed inwardly, by the second outwardly, by the third highest, and by the fourth lowest.

Reviving

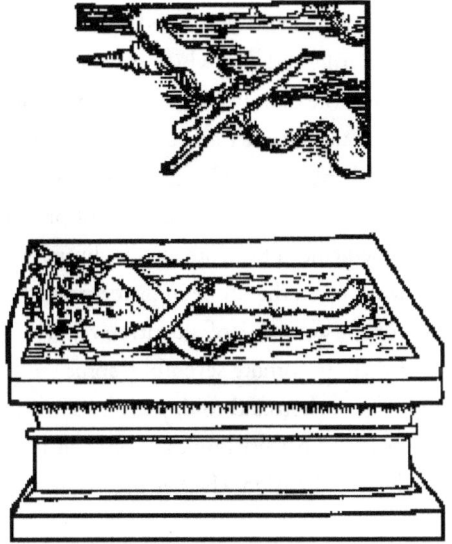

>Here the Soul descendeth gloriously from heaven,
>And raiseth up the Daughter of Philosophy.

Geber in his third book and 19th Chapter: Because we have fully entreated of the known experiences of the sufficiency of the causes of this magistery, according to the exigency of speech concerning our purpose, now it remains for us to come in one little chapter to the accomplishment of the whole divine work and to draw the dispersed magistery into a brevity of speech.

We say therefore because there is no brief intention of the whole work but that the known stone may be taken, and then with the instances of the work the sublimation to be continued upon it, and by this it is cleansed from the corrupting impurity and it is the perfection of sublimation and with it the stone is to be made subtle until it come into the last purity of subtleness, and lastly be made volatile. But from hence let it be fixed with the manners of fixing, until it wax quiet in the sharpness of the fire and here consists the second degree of preparation.

And in the third degree the stone is administered in like sort which consists in the last accomplishment of the preparation, that is to say that you make the Stone which is now fixed with the means of Sublimation, to be volatile, and that which is volatile to be fixed, and the fixed dissolved, and the dissolved to be again volatile, and again to make the volatile fixed until it melt and alter in the sure accomplishment of Sol and Luna. Therefore the multiplication of the goodness of alteration rejoices at the reiteration of preparation of the third degree in the medicine. Therefore, of the diversity of the reiteration of the work upon the Stone in his degrees, the diversity of the multiplication of the goodness of alteration rejoices, that of the medicines some of them transmute sevenfold, some tenfold, some an hundred fold and some a thousand fold, yea, and some transmute infinitely into the true and perfect bodies of Sol and Luna. From hence, therefore, and lastly, let it be tried whether the magistery consists in perfection.

Therefore let him attend who desires to know the properties of the action, or the manner of the composition of the greater Elixir, for we speak to make one substance yet gathered out of many united together and fixed, which being put upon the fire, the fire may not alter it, and being mingled with melted things it may melt with them, it may be mingled with that which is of an ingrossable substance in it and with that which is of a mingling substance, and is hardened with that which is of an hard substance and fixed with that which is of an fixing substance, and it is not burnt of these things that burn gold or silver, and brings to the consolidation with a due and perfect fieryness.

Yet you may not understand it so far in a short time, when in a four days or hours it may be restored at the first turn, but that in respect of the modern physicians and in respect also of the truth of the operation of nature, but this is sooner ended. From whence the Philosopher has said, "A medicine is that which in the long space of time has been anticipated," wherefore I tell you that you labour patiently because it is a necessity so to do, and surely hastiness is partly of the Devil.

Therefore he who has no patience, let him refrain his hands from the work, because unbelief hinders him by reason of his hastiness.

For every action naturally has its mean and determined time, in which space more or less it is determined.

There are three things necessary for this Art, that is Patience, Delay and Aptness of instruments, of which we have spoken in diverse chapters in the sum of this perfect magistery, in which we conclude with manifest and open proof, that our Stone is nothing else but a stinking spirit and a living water which we also name dry water, and cleansed by natural proportion and united with such union, that it cannot be separated from it. To which the third ought to be added, to abbreviate the work this perfect body is attenuated.

Therefore from the premises, the things are manifest, in which the truth consists and by which the work itself is effected.

Of the Coagulation and Preparation of the First Stone and the Sublimation of it

Here follows certain more notable things collected out of a little book of one called Ademarus upon Geber the King of the Persians, and in the fourth chapter where he says -

As much as the Stone is cleansed by sublimation and by its burning taken away by the extraction of the oil from it, and his flight is destroyed by the fixing of it, yet nevertheless it is neither melted, entered into, nor mingled, but it is vitrified, as it is in the seventh chapter of Geber. Yea, rather it ought to be dissolved in the sharpness of waters and be calcined many times as it is had in the sixty seventh chapter of Geber.

Geber in his sixth chapter says that by the manifold reiteration of Imbibing and with light grinding and drying the wateriness of it, the greater part is blotted out. This is therefore the Sublimation of the first degree, by which the wateriness of Mercury is consumed afterwards in a vessel body which is described in the twenty eighth chapter, that whole substance must be sprinkled in the bottom of it and then let the fire be increased as it is said in the third chapter about the middle of it, until part of it excelling pure in whiteness the white snow, sticks to the brims of the body, his whiteness being as it were dead. And this is our Sublimation by which the earthly stinkingness and the parts of Sulphur with the faeces remain at the bottom, and in it its nature is purified, and from hence let it be fixed with the manner of fixing, that is fermented, and then let it be set in dung. It follows until it wax quiet in the sharpness of the fire, and this is called the second Degree of preparation that is of Sublimation, but if it be demanded how Mercury may be subtilated when in act it hath a most subtle substance (as is said in the thirty ninth and seventy third chapters), where it is said that it should be cleansed and subtilated by the manner of sublimation or subtilation that is with sublimation of the first degree. Therefore lastly let it stand volatile, that is let it be sublimed with firing, so that it may ascend from the faeces as clear as crystal to the brims of the vessel.

Geber says "make white Laton, that is earth, and lay up the books, that your hearts may not be broken". And in another place: "Fire and water do wash Laton, and wipe away the blackness of it". It follows therefore that which is sublimed in the vessel Aludel, reiterate it one time, that is fix it by subliming, as he says in his sixty-second chapter, because a soft fire as it is said in the same place is a preserver of the moistness and a perfecter of the fusion. Likewise it is said in the thirtieth chapter that Argent vive ought first to be sublimed and afterwards to be fixed.

Likewise it is said in the twenty-eighth chapter that Mercury is fixed by his successive sublimation, so that it may give metallic fusion or melting. You shall find this self same thing oftentimes in his sayings. All these aforesaid things ought to be understood of the preparation of the first Stone and the whitening of it, before the putting of it in dung because it must be so often incerated with sharp waters and be dissolved and coagulated upon ashes, until it wax to soft and white and in the end flow like bright Luna. For this is the sublimation of it, that is into an higher dignity and virtue, and this is his true purification.

It follows in the seventh chapter, but I counsel thee that thou begin this work with imperfect stones for this hath been of the principal and hidden understanding of that Geber. So you have in the seventeenth chapter that the nature of Mercury is so in bodies as it is in Mercury, yes in Mercury, yea rather it is most perfect in known stones. Likewise it is said in the third chapter that the nature of mortified Mercury is in Marcasite and meanly prepared which is of more force. That Philosopher in his works, only means the nature of Mercury, but the whole nature of Sol is of Mercury as it is said in the eighth chapter.

Likewise that Philosopher will have that substance of Mercury mortified, but naturally the Mercury of it is in that honourable Stone, as it is manifest to all men.

Likewise that Philosopher will have that substance of Mercury fixed as it is manifest because he teaches the policies of fixing with wariness and warnings but who would doubt the substance of that most precious Stone to be fixable, surely no man that knows it.

Likewise the Philosopher will have his stone to be fixed with the heat of the fire, that the moistness of it may be preserved, but where is there a more temperate heat than in the bowels of the earth. Likewise the Philosopher will have his stone to be melted, therefore it is manifest that the Stone is master of the Philosophers, as if he should say that he does that even naturally by himself which he is held to do, and so the Philosopher is not master of the Stone but rather its minister.

Therefore, he seeks by art beyond nature, by artifice to induce some matter into the thing which is not naturally in it, does err greatly and shall bewail his error.

Sol is the beginning for the red work, and Luna for the white work, being purged from its burning and combustible sulphur.

But that there is in it such a substance, you have in the forty-seventh chapter, and that Luna is the Stone for the white work, you have in the eighteenth chapter.

Take therefore this most precious Stone, having body, soul and spirit, and calcine it with its moisture, or with Mercury, so that it may not be touched in it.

But the Stone is administered even in the third degree which consists in the last accomplishment of the preparation, and it is that thou make the Stone, which is now fixed by means of Sublimation, to be volatile, and sublime it with the spirits not fixed. The fixed to be sublimed is nothing else than for the body to be converted into a spirit which secret is thus extracted out of the sayings of the Philosophers, for it is had in the thirty-seventh chapter that the spirit is not mingled to the body, that is to the fixed substance, whatsoever it be, unless the Stone be first dissolved, and coagulated with the Magistery, but if you demand how the Stone may be dissolved, we must say that it is done with strong waters having briny bitterness and sharpness, being without faeces, as the vinegar of wine is.

But if you demand why the Stone should be dissolved, we must say as is said in the thirty-seventh chapter, that everything that is dissolved getteth the nature of Salts and Alums, because salts only are first melted before they are vitrified, and likewise according to their nature those salts only are dissolved. If therefore our Stone be dissolved then it gets the nature of Salts, but that which is melted is ingrediated, and whatsoever does enter into, the same also transmuteth. It is said in the fifty-seventh chapter that bodies are sublimed by the most excellent degree of the fire until the fixed be wholly lifted up with the unfixed as it is in the twelfth chapter, but if the whole of it be not sublimed, then add a quantity of the unfixed part to it, until it suffice for the total elevation. By most strong fire, understand the fire of putrefaction, and of our Mercury, by the which only the body is elevated, that is, converted into a spirit. Therefore when it shall be lifted up, reiterate his

Sublimation until the whole be fixed by the administration of reiteration. And make the fixed dissolved, that is, put it to vinegar as before, by reiterating all four times as it hath sufficiently been declared, and make the dissolved volatile as if he should say that by Solution the Stone is made volatile and again make the volatile fixed. He useth these words in his fifty-seventh chapter, as long as it yieldeth fusion and melteth, and in the tenth chapter "Is this the Work for the white or for the red?"

Adamarus answers for both, for so it is written in the sixty-sixth chapter, that the Lunary and Solary Stone are all in one essence, because each of them is effected by means of Mercury only. There is also one way in manner of doing it, because it is done by the same operations and with the same order, therefore it is one medicine according to all Philosophers, yet they differ in fermentation.

The Demonstration of Perfection

The Riddle of the King:

Here is born the king of all glory
There cannot be any created
Greater in the world than he
Neither by Art nor Nature
Of what living creature soever
The Philosophers call him their son
He effecteth all things which they do
And whatsoever men expect of him
He giveth continual health
Gold, Silver and precious stones
He giveth fortitude, long life, beauty
And Purity. He expelleth Anger,
Sorrow, Poverty and diseases
Blessed is he on whom God bestows this gift.

The Answer of Luna the Queen:

Here is born a noble and a rich Queen
Whom the Philosophers liken unto their Daughter
She multiplies and brings forth infinite Children
Free from all hurt impurity and spot
She expells death and hates poverty
She gives wealth, health, honour
And all good things
She excells Gold, Silver and precious stones
And all medicines both precious and simple
There is nothing on the whole face of the Earth
That may be compared unto her
For which give endless thanks to the great God of Heaven.

Geber: We are certain by our investigation and we have considered by manifest experiences that all these words are true which have been written by us only in our volumes, and secondly we have seen those things by trial and reason which we have brought into those volumes, but we have written those things in the Sum of the Perfection of our magistery, which we by our experiences have extracted with our fingers, seen with our eyes and felt with our hands, therefore let the wise artificer study in our volumes by gathering together our dispersed intention which we have set down in divers places with the intent that it should not be made common to the wicked and ignorant. And let him prove that which he collects by studying and experimenting with politic instance of labour until he attain to the full knowledge. Therefore, let the Artificer exercise himself and he shall find. But we, to the intent we may avoid the slanders of the envious, will declare it, because we have not delivered our science and knowledge by the continuance of speech, but we have sprinkled it in diverse little chapters and to this intent, because if it should have been delivered in continuance of speech, the improbate as well as the honest would unworthily have usurped it. And for this cause, where we have spoken most plainly there we have most of all concealed and hidden it, yet not under riddles and dark questions, but we have spoken unto the artificer under plain order of speech and have delivered it in the order of talk. Let not, therefore, the Son of Learning despair, because if he seek it he shall find it, because he that shall seek it by the goodness of his own industry shall find out the science, but he that shall seek it by the following of books shall very slowly attain to this most precious art, because we have declared this art only to ourselves and to no other, being found out by ourselves only that most true and altogether certain, since we have expounded unto them the way of investigation delivered unto us, but we have written that which is found to none but to ourselves only, but the manner of searching and policy of means. Therefore, let the workman that is of a good mind exercise himself by these things which we have delivered and he shall rejoice that he hath found out the gift of the most high God. Therefore, let these words suffice for the full searching out of this most excellent art. So far the words of Geber.

Geber in his Summary in the sixteenth chapter of natural principles says thus, for we must note that after the Stone shall be purified and perfectly cleansed from everything corrupting it, and after it shall be fermented, you shall not need any more to change your vessel, nor to open it, but only to pray that God may preserve it from breaking, and for this cause the Philosopher said, that in one vessel the whole magistery is effected. And you must know that in forty days and nights the work is accomplished for white after the true purification of the Stone, because in the preparation there can be no determined time unless the artificer labour well, and in ninety days and nights the work is accomplished for the red. And these are the true times for the full perfection. Understand this concerning Coagulation which is done after purification, which purification hath nothing else to be done but in the putrefaction and conversion of the body into a mere spirit, and when thou shalt have this, praise God.

Senior: I am Luna, increasing moist and cold, and thou art Sol, hot and moist (otherwise dry). When we shall be coupled in equity of state in a mansion which is not made otherwise but with light fire, having with itself great heat in which we shall be emptied, and we shall be as a woman that wants the fruit of her increase, and Sol and myself when we shall be conjoined we shall be emptied in the belly of the house being shut, I will by flattery take thy soul from thee, if thou take away my beauty and comely shape, we shall rejoice and shall be exalted by the rejoicing of the spirit when we shall ascend the order of the aged, then the light of thy light shall be poured into my light, and of thee and me there is a commixtion made of wine and sweet water, and I forbid my melting after thou shalt have put on blackness with my colour, which is like ink after my solution and coagulation. When we shall enter into the house of love, my body shall be coagulated and I shall be in my emptiness.

Sol answers saying: If thou do this and wilt not hurt me, O Luna, my body shall be changed and afterwards I will give unto thee a new virtue of penetrating by which thou shalt be mighty in the virtue of the fire of liquefaction and purging, out of which thou shalt go forth without any diminishing or blackness, as copper and lead, and thou shalt not be resisted, when as thou art not weak. These are the words of Adamalus.

Raymund Lully in his Epistle to Rupert, King of France
You must know that there is a certain oil of a golden colour extracted out of the Lead of the Philosophers, with which, if you shall sublime a mineral stone, a vegetable or an animal, after the first fixtion three or four times, it will excuse you from all labour of Solutions and Coagulations. The reason is because this is hidden which makes the medicine penetrable, friendly and conjoinable with all, and it will augment the effect thereof beyond measure, so that in the world there is not a more secret thing.

Wherefore I speak things which are miraculous, which seemed to be incredible to all the ancient Philosophers, that is, that thou shalt know well to separate this oil from the wateriness and thou shalt labour in the manner of the mixtion of them, and thou shalt be able to make the Stone in 30 days, but this is not necessary by itself because the solutions and coagulations of it (as hath been said) are quickly made and done.

But if the Sublimation of it should be made, I believe the tincture of the Stone would be much enlarged. Out of these things therefore choose your purpose. The reason of Galen whereupon Ixir or Elixir is made and he says that diverse teachers put diverse medicines. Some say that Ixir is of the minerals of mountains, some say of herbs, some of beasts and urine. But it is made of one of those things, which is put in an Alembic, and first the water comes forth in fume that is the spirit, secondly Oil in liquor, that is the Soul, but the third which remains in the vessel is earthly and it is called the body, for of those three, spirit, soul and body, Ixir is made being so decocted that it may be mingled and melted. Some say that Sulphur and Argent vive will become Ixir if a man make them fusible.

Note that neither water, nor oil, nor fire, hath his efficacy to tinct, but it is first rectified by reiteration of reduction to the faeces and distillations. We add even 8 to 10 times therefore, in all things as well to be dissolved or fixed or tincted, or in any thing to be effected there is a mean to be observed, because that intention in due order doth ornament and accomplish a thing, that is to say that imperfect bodies be duly calcined subtly washed and mollified, imbibed or cerated and put to solution in manner aforsaid. But let the spirits be subtly washed and purified and let them be put to mollification and humiliation, and let those things that are hot and dry be dissolved, calcined or sublimed according to that he shall see and it is judged better according to the sound sense of the working.

I am the true green and Golden Lion without cares,
In me all the secrets of the Philosophers are hidden.

Of Our Mercury which is the Green Lion Devouring the Sun
Know that it is Mercury cold and moist and God hath created all minerals of it, for it is an airy element, flying from the fire. Therefore, when any part is fixed to it, it effecteth an high matter and it is a profitable spirit, and there is not any thing in the world but it. Neither is there any thing that may stand in the place of it, and it is a thing searching to the bottom in every body, and enriching it. Therefore, when it is mingled with the body, it reviveth it and illuminates it and converts it from disposition to disposition, and, from one colour into another, therefore it is the whole Elixir of whiteness and redness, and it is a permanent water, and water of life and death, it is virgin's milk, the herb of washing and the animal fountain, of which whosoever drinks

dies not, and it is susceptive of colour and a medicine of them causing them to take colours, and it is that which mortifies, dries, moistens and makes hot and cold, and it does contrary things according to the measure of its regimen, and when it is quick it hath other operations, and when it is dead it hath other operations of others, and when it is sublimed there are other operations unto it. And he is a Dragon which marries himself and does impregnate himself and he brings forth in his day, and kills all animals with his poison, and the fire destroys him, and it destroys in short time by reason of the Argent vive. Neither can he overcome it, nor eat it, but flies from it. The former wise philosophers have bethought themselves of the means of policies belonging unto it, until by little and little it be made abiding the fire, therefore it does not cease to be graduated upon the fight of the fire, and it is fed of it, so that when any fixion is fixed to it, wonderful and strange mutations happen because when it is changed it changes, and his blackness appears and his sound and his brightness, therefore when it is tincted, it is tincted and it tincteth; when it is dissolved, it is dissolved and it dissolveth, and it whiteneth in the sight of the eye and it maketh red in succession, and it is a water gathering together, and it is milk and strong urine and mollifying oil and the father of all miracles, and it is a mist and a cloud and fugitive servant, and occidental Mercury, which hath preferred himself before Gold and hath overcome it. Therefore Gold says unto him, dost thou prefer thyself before me, And I am Lord of Stones enduring the fire. Our Mercury says unto it, but I have begat thee and thou art born of me, and one part of me revives many parts of thee, but thou art covetous and givest not any thing in comparison to me, and he which shall bind me with my brother and my sister shall live and rejoice, and it shall suffice him in all his life, if he should live a thousand thousand years, and every day sustain seven thousand men, yet he should never want, and I am the whole secret and in me the Science is hidden, because I convert all bodies into Sol and Luna, when my nature is such that I mollify the hard, and make the soft hard. And therefore note that the Philosophers' Stone for the true Alchemy itself is this thing only in the whole world, and he which errs in this one thing is thought to run headlong from the matter, but yet it is not perfect in his nature, to which workmanship itself has brought it, for without the magistery it is of no force with us nor of any commodity, neither does it perfectly yield any thing but rather corrupteth, and this therefore I speak so far forth as you use it with the magistery because it is pure phlegm. Sometimes the Philosophers call it Sulphur and melancholy citrine, by reason of the effect of his miraculous virtue, for as some men will have it, of it God created all nations and appointed the original of them for some men have called this our stone, white copper.

Whereupon Lucas and Eximenus say, understand all you that search after knowledge, that no tincture is made but of our white copper. For our copper is not common copper. Common copper is corrupted and infecteth everything which is put unto it, but the Copper of Philosophers maketh perfect and whiteneth that to which it is associated.

Therefore Plato says, all gold is copper, but all copper is not gold, therefore our copper has body, soul and spirit, and these three are one, from one, and with one, which is the root of it, therefore the copper of the Philosophers is their Elixir accomplished and perfected of body, soul and spirit. So the Philosophers have named the Stone by diverse names that it might be manifest to the wise and hidden from the ignorant, but by what name soever it is named, yet is it always one and the same thing.

Whereupon Merculinus says:

It is an hidden stone and buried in a deep fountain
And cast in the ways and covered with dirt or dung
This one Stone hath all names
Whereupon Morienus, that godly man, says:
This Stone is a Stone and no Stone
It is a bird and no bird
It is Jupiter, Mars, Sol, Venus,
And Luna

Now silver, now gold and now an element
Now water, now wine, now blood
Now virgin's milk, now spume of the sea or vinegar
Now Sal Gemme, now common salt
Now auripigmentum
Now the purged sea purified with Sulphur
And thus they figure it because they would not reveal it to the Ignorant
Nor conceal it from those that be wise
And that the Copper which is handled be not distributed to fools
This only Luna is called by all names

And these are the orders of the operations of this Stone by the help of which this thing which we seek is engendered and is brought into actual essence.

And Sublimation is one means, Descension another, Distillation the third Calcination the fourth, Solution the fifth, Congelation the sixth, Fixion the seventh, Iteration the eighth, Ceration the ninth and many more like these they recite, which orders surely although they be diverse in reason, yet they are all one in matter, for sometimes the Philosophers considering the matter of them which when it is in the vessel and feels the Sun or the heat incontinently and breathes and evaporates away into the form of most subtle fume, and ascends into the head of the vessel. And this they have called Ascension and Sublimation. Afterwards, they seeing the matter which ascended to descend to the bottom of the vessel, they have called it Distillation or Descension, moreover they seeing that substance or matter to thicken and wax black and to give an evil savour, they have called it Putrefaction. They seeing a black and dark colour and perceiving it after a long time to cast forth an evil smell and a little whiteness to come like the colour of ashes, they have called it Inceration or Dealbation.

Morienus: The whole magistery is nothing else but an extraction of water out of earth, and a casting of water upon the earth until it be putrified and this earth putrefies with water, and when it shall be cleansed, then by the help of him which ruleth all things, the whole magistery is effected. Moreover they seeing the earth to be mingled with the water, and the water little by little to be diminished by reason of his temperate decoction and the earth to increase, they have all said this to be perfect Ceration. Whereupon the Philosopher says that the earth is Cerated, Imbibed, and by the temperate decoction of the Sun, that is of the heat, it is dried with the water and the whole matter is turned into earth.

Whereupon Morienus says, this is the pure and full force if it be turned into earth.

Lastly, they seeing that the whole matter came into a certain dissipation and how it reduced itself to a hard substance, and because it melted not but stood strictly, they have said that this was perfect Congelation.

Whereupon Plato says, dissolve our Stone and afterwards Congeal it with great wariness as it has been demonstrated unto you, and you shall have as it were the whole magistery. The same man says in another place, Take our Stone and put it in a vessel and dry it with a light fire until it be broken and afterwards decoct it at the heat of the Sun until it be congealed, and know that the whole magistery is nothing else but to make true solution and perfect and natural congelation. These are the words of Plato.

Plato also says, Dissolve and Congeal and thus you shall know the whole magistery. Likewise they seeing the aforesaid matter perfectly congealed and thickened, so that by no means it resolved itself any more into water, nor into fume, they have said that it was truly fixed, because they saw that congelation and thickness or fixion, by reason of the greater decoction of heat, to come into perfect dryness and whiteness, and because that whiteness was beyond all other whiteness, therefore they have said that this was perfect Calcination. They seeing this matter to stand to its colour and to be changed with infinite colours, because this could not be done but by the resolution of the matter therefore they called this resolution Solution, for the elements are discontinuated with that resolution, and they die and suffer. And therefore the Philosophers call these elements, Man and Wife, wherefore, the foolish and ignorant are shamefully deceived who believe that the Philosophers' medicine is created out of any other thing, when as the Philosophers say. "The Sons of Alchemy and others trusting to all their Dissolutions, Sublimations, Conjunctions, Separations, Congelations, Preparations, Contritions and other deceits, vaunt themselves saying that there is no other Gold but theirs, no other water but theirs, which is also called most sharp vinegar, no other Dissolution and Congelation but theirs, which is made with a soft fire, no other putrefaction but theirs."

Plato in his Summary: Therefore let thy seeking be of the kind of both of the lights of the world, for Gold circumpasses the upper part and Silver the lower part.

Aristotle: No tincting poison is engendered without Sol and his shadow that is his wife.

Hermes in his secrets: Sol is his father and Luna his mother.

Rosarius: Whosoever endeavours to seek any other tincture without Sol and Luna, he is likened to a man that would climb a ladder without steps, therefore it is necessary that we have our receptacle fit for tincture, which is agreeable unto it, with a certain similitude unto the Father, and this receptacle ought to be Luna herself, because Sol of itself is of very hard fusion or melting, and in like sort Luna by itself, but when they are joined both together, then they both flow and melt very easily, and thus therefore the Goldsmiths make their solders.

The Philosopher: The woman is a certain receptacle of the seed of the man, because she preserves it and keeps it in her Cell and Matrix and there it is nourished and grows even to the time of his ripeness, therefore let us now choose unto him a wife, that he may have a receptacle of his seed, whom we may choose for the wife, which is nearer to him in simplicity and purity, because nothing is more near to the man than the wife which are homogenous.

Hermes says in his Allegories: Luna is the light of the night, the night is the nativity of Darkness, which God has ordained for the governing of the world. And Luna receives her Light from Sol and is beloved, because the light of Sol is in her and because the nature of Sol overcomes the nature of Luna. Our Mercury is made of a mineral and vegetable joined together, because things joined together do profit more, than if they should be separated by themselves, out of those things consider the necessity of both Mercuries.

Democritus the Philosopher: It behoves you that in the first business you dissolve the bodies upon white ashes and let there be no grinding but with water.

Avicenna: The first thing in the work is to dissolve the Stone into his first matter.

Senior and Hermes: Dissolve the bodies into waters.

Plato in his Summary: Thou wantest that which thou labourest for in the Solution of bodies therefore it is meet to continue a gentle fire upon it until all the whole be dissolved, and by it the work is effected.

Note this, the circulatory reversion of all circulary things is not effected until they be brought unto their first matter.

Rasis: Unless you dissolve the bodies you labour in vain.

Albertus Magnus: Know for a certainty that no spirit of bodies can be tincted unless it first be dissolved.

Morienus: The operation is vain in this Art unless all natural things pass into vapour by their nature, and if it shall be dissolved then the alchemical work is prepared and multiplied.

Sorin in his 11th Distinction: Perfect Solution is the beginning of the regimen, but that the body may wax thin like unto a spirit, then it is meet to dissolve them and the regimen of bodies, as I have said before, is dissolved.

Alphidius: But Argent vive which is extracted from that black body is moist and white and clean from barks, that the work perish not.

Morienus: It is convenient for thee to know that white fume is the soul and spirit of those dissolved bodies, and surely if white fume had not been Gold, there Alchemy had not been.

Rosanius: This is our most notable Mercury and God never created a more notable thing under heaven beside a rational soul.

Hermes King of the Grecians: The dissolved body is continual water congealing Mercury with perpetual congelation.

Hipocras: He that will purge bodies must first make them fluxible, the blackness of putrefaction according to the opinion of some men lasts 4 or 5 days.

Senior: The first key is the extraction of moistures and fatness, of which these are the signs, that is to say, superabundant blackness which being consumed, the soul is now in the water.

Albertus: Unless the soul shall come forth from the body and shall ascend upward into heaven, you shall profit nothing in this art.

Senior, the Parable concerning the White Tincture: If my beloved parents shall taste of life and shall be fed with mere milk and shall be made drunk with my white, and shall lie in my bed, they shall beget the Son of Luna which shall excell all his predecessors, and if my beloved shall carry him from the red tomb of rock and shall taste of the fountain of his mother, and shall be coupled with my red wine and shall be made drunk with me, and shall couple with me freely in his bed, and in my love his sperm shall enter into my cell, I shall conceive and be pregnant and at my time will bring forth a most mighty Son ruling and reigning over all kings and princes of the earth, crowned with a golden crown of victory, of the most high God who lives and reigns world without end.

The Turba of the Philosophers: You searchers of this Art when you see that whiteness appearing in all places of the glass, then imagine that redness is hidden in that whiteness, and then you must not extract it until the whole red be made to decoct.

Senior: Make black white, and every white red, because water whitens and fire illuminates, for it shines in colour like a ruby by a tincting soul, which it hath gotten by virtue of the fire.

Hermes: The seventh regimen is of Luna, that is, to dry to make red, to make hot and to fix by the space of 25 days and so you have the finishing of the work. The colour of the soul is red. White will be red. Whiteness is our redness. Likewise, this our Stone is fire and created of fire, and turned into fire, and the soul of it stays in the fire.

The Riddle of Hermes Concerning the Red Tincture: I am crowned, and decked with a precious crown and adorned with princely garments, for that I cause joy to enter into bodies.

Hermes in his Third Treatise: Come ye Sons of Wisdom and now we will rejoice and be merry together, because death is conquered and our Son now reigneth and is clothed with a red ornament and with flesh. Now our Son being born a King, takes the tincture from the fire, but death the Sea and darkness fly from him, and the Dragon flies the beams of the Sun which kept the holes, and our Son being dead doth live, and a King comes from the fire and shall rejoice in wedlock and secret things shall appear, and our Son now vivified is made a warrior in the fire and supereminent in tinctures.

The Metaphor of Bellinus the Philosopher concerning Sol: Know thee that my father Sol hath given me power over all power and hath put on me the garment of glory and the whole world seeketh me and runneth after me, for I am the greatest now they have known my virtue and altitude, for I am only and alone which of his grace has given me that virtue, and men seek of my servants that which is sought of me, and they have not come unto it but through me, and the earth with all her forces cannot make me humble myself. Yea, rather I am above it and above my servants, until I humble them and extract from the nature and power of them, and endue them with my brightness and fair light which my father hath given unto me in all their works, for I am excelling, which exalt and surpass all things and none of my servants can be above me but one to whom it is granted because he is contrary to me, and he destroys me, yet he destroys not my nature, and that is Saturn who separates all my members. Afterwards I go to my mother who gathers together all my divided and separated members. I am illuminating all my things and I cause light to appear manifestly in the journey of my father Saturn, and also of my mother who is an enemy unto me. But if this should not be, I could not drink of the souls of animals and of plants, but I come with the heat of the fire to expell the virtue and iniquity of them from me. I am dwelling upon the face of the mineral and I give to my servants of my extremities, and my name is called by great names and he that studies in me cares not for any thing, but he is not satisfied with me. I carry ships through the sea and I build great cities and towers, seek not in me my greatness, therefore you wise men I tell you that unless you kill me your undertaking shall not be perfect and the degree of your wisdom increases in my sister Luna, and not with any of my servants. And if you should know my secret, I am seed cast into pure earth, which growing increases and multiplies and it brings forth fruit to him that sows it, because every thing that is engendered with his kind, doth multiply the form of his own shape and of no other, as of corn there comes corn, and so of other things, and in this I have expounded all the figures. Therefore, when I shall be with my white pure moist and clean wife, I add to the beauty of her face, to her goodness and virtue, for she is obedient unto me. Therefore, when I shall be joined unto her, there is nothing more excellent and better in the world, for she shall be impregnated and shall grow and she shall be as I am in substance and colour, because by this magistery the seed is multiplied, for of me, my like is born, and when one grain of corn is sown in the ground, it springs and is multiplied, grinded and seared, and is made into bread, of which the whole world lives. And the mineral of the earth is made of me, neither does it because it is the gift of God. I illuminate the air with my light and make the earth hot with my heat. I engender and nourish natural things, as plants and stones and such like. I take away the darkness of the night with my power, and I cause the days to remain and I illuminate all things with my light that are to be illuminated, and those things in which there is neither greatness nor brightness, all which surely are of my work when I am endued with my garments, and they which seek me do make peace between me and my wife. Therefore, unless she be separated from me and be mixed with inseparable mixtion, and this may be done when you shall extract me partly from my nature and my wife partly from her nature, and afterwards see that you kill our natures, and we shall be raised again with a new and incorporeal resurrection, because that afterwards we cannot die, for after our resurrection we shall have everlasting glory and fortitude and then all shall rejoice in great prosperity which know our proceedings.

And in this is the most precious gift of God accomplished, which exceeds all secrets of sciences in the world, and it is an incomparable treasure of treasures, because Plato says he that hath this gift of God hath also the dominion of the world, because he hath attained to riches and has broken the bond of nature, but not therefore because he has the power to connect all imperfect bodies into most pure Sol and Luna, but rather because it preserves and keeps every man and brute beast in perfect preservation of health, and the crystal plate which is the White Elixir, if as much thereof as a grain of mustard seed be given to a man sick of the fever, it cures him. Likewise a leprous man, if at four times in the year he shall be purged with that plate, with red powder whereof Sol is made twice in one year in March and September, he is cured. And both the white and the red powder heals the Sciatica in the danger of death it heals also the palsy. Likewise if this be held to the nostrils of women labouring with child they are presently delivered, this Hermes affirms.

Geber also says that the red Elixir cures all cronical infirmities of which the Physicians have despaired, and it makes a man become young as an eagle and to live five hundred years and more, as some Philosophers have done, which have used it three times a week to the quantity of a mustard seed. There is an herb which is called Saturnus de Canalibus, of which such a medicine is made.

Note therefore that all infirmities which are engendered from the crown of the head to the sole of the foot, if they be of one month, then they are cured in one day, if of one year then in twelve days, and if of long time then they are cured in one month, for as it cleanses all infected metals from all infirmity, so likewise it cures the bodies of men.

Wherefore, our blessed Stone is not unworthily called the greater Tiriacus, as well of the bodies of men as of metals, of which Hermes, the King of the Grecians and father of the Philosophers, speaks saying, if thou takes of our Elixir every day for the space of seven years the weight of carrobiarum, thy hoary and grey hairs will fall from thy head and black hairs will grow up in their place, and thus of an old man thou shalt be made young, lusty and strong.

Arnoldus: This our Stone has an efficacious virtue of healing all infirmities above all other medicines of Physicians, for it rejoices the Soul, it augmenteth virtue, it strengthens youth and removes old age, for it suffers not the blood to be putrefied, nor phlegm to have dominion, nor choler to be adust, nor melancholiness to be abundant, yea rather it multiplies the blood beyond measure and restores and renews all corporeal members efficaciously and preserves them from hurt, and does most perfectly heal all infirmities, as well hot as cold, dry as moist, before all other medicines of Physicians, because if the sickness be of one year, it heals it in twelve days but if it be an old disease and of long time then it will cure it in one month, and to conclude it expells all evil humours and brings in those that are good, it brings love, honour, security, boldness, and victory in battle to those that possess it and in this is the greatest secret of nature accomplished which is,

>A secret not to be valued at any price
>a most precious and incomparable treasure
>which God grant to be hidden
>in their minds that possess it
>lest it be made known
>to the foolish
>and ignorant
>
>Amen let every
>living man say
>
>Finis
>
>In Lubeck the 24th day of the
>month of October in the year
>of our Lord 1588

After my passion and manifold torments I am again risen,
Being purified and cleansed from all spots.

www.ingramcontent.com/pod-product-compliance
Lightning Source LLC
Chambersburg PA
CBHW071218160426
43196CB00012B/2343